# breddos
# TACOS
## the COOKBOOK

# breddos TACOS

## the COOKBOOK

**RECIPES BY NUD DUDHIA**
**STORIES BY CHRIS WHITNEY**

PHOTOGRAPHY BY KRIS KIRKHAM

quadrille

**Publishing director**  Sarah Lavelle
**Creative director**  Helen Lewis
**Junior commissioning editor**  Romilly Morgan
**Art direction & design**  Alexander Green
**Design assistant**  Emily Lapworth
**Food & reportage photographer**  Kris Kirkham
**Documentary photographer**  Ronni Campana (gloss insert section)
**Production**  Tom Moore, Vincent Smith

First published in 2016 by
Quadrille Publishing
Pentagon House
52–54 Southwark Street
London SE1 1UN
www.quadrille.co.uk
www.quadrille.com

Quadrille is an imprint of Hardie Grant
www.hardiegrant.com.au

Cataloguing in Publication Data: a catalogue record
for this book is available from the British Library.

ISBN: 978 184949 799 2

Printed in China

# CONTENTS

## INTRODUCTION:
## 2 BREDDOS, 1 SHACK, 1 DREAM

After many years of living in London together, being disillusioned with our professions and having food ideas that never came to fruition, we got talking about tacos, or rather the lack of good ones in our area. Ideas were discussed, but this time, for whatever reason, it seemed to be more than idle chat. The decision was made in the pub after six pints (as all the best ones are), we were going to start a taco stall. First things first, we needed a name...

'Breddos' is a bastardized, slang word that originates from the term 'brethren'. It's an expression we coined whilst we were at university to refer to our friends. Fifteen years later, when we decided to build a makeshift taco shack in an abandoned car park in Hackney, East London, we couldn't think of a better name, and so breddos Tacos was born. We started with no real understanding of what we were getting ourselves into nor what we wanted to achieve. Little did we know what lay in store over the next couple of years...

The ritual before we started breddos Tacos was to leave our respective jobs as early as humanly possible on Friday evening (much like the rest of the right-thinking world...) and we would settle into some pints at The Cat & Mutton on Broadway Market in Hackney. We'd sit there until closing, setting the world to rights with our friends. Broadway Market is famous for its Saturday market but it's also home to several others. Netil market was based in a derelict car park with a couple of food traders and assorted stalls of oddments. After a short email application we were granted permission to build a shack, and before we knew it, we had a 2 x 3 metres (6½ x 10 feet) taco shack. This is when things began to take shape. Recipe tests were carried out, funny moments ensued, arguments were had; a particularly memorable one was when we realized a week before opening that neither of us had the faintest idea of how to roll a burrito.

When the first day of trading snuck up on us, we had written list upon list to ensure that nothing was overlooked, every eventuality planned for, and that nothing could faze us. We opened the hatch, ready for business. Our first customer arrived, it was really

happening! Until we realized that we'd overlooked a <u>tiny</u> detail. We'd forgotten to buy tortillas...

We soon developed a Friday night schedule for our slow-cooked short-rib tacos. Whoever arrived home from work first would go to the Ginger Pig Butcher in Victoria Park and buy the ribs, then on to the shack, in order to marinate them. This done, we would head to the pub. At about 10 p.m., the time came to prepare the ribs and start cooking them, so that they'd be perfectly ready for midday on Saturday. Access to our little shack at this time of night was slightly precarious. The gates were always locked and so we'd have to jump over a 2-metre (6½ foot)

wall. Now, due to the fact we had been sitting in the pub most of the evening, there was the added element of drunken ineptitude to contend with. Once we'd scaled the wall, we'd fumble our way to the shack and prepare the ribs. One of us would prep the broth and the other would sear the ribs and get them into the slow cookers. We'd always have an argument or three during this time of the night, normally about overcooking the onions or failing to adhere to a recipe. Once the slow cookers were set up we would retire and get a good night's sleep before getting up at the crack of dawn to begin preparing for an afternoon of trading.

During these first few weeks we only had one slow cooker, which was enough to cook 2-3kg (4½-6½lb) of short-rib. But, as we started to gain loyal customers who visited us week in, week out, we noticed that we started to sell out earlier each time. This was great as it meant we could adjourn to the pub early. On the other hand, with the hope that this might turn into an actual business, it was pretty stupid to be turning people away. We needed to expand...

First off, we bought a couple more slow cookers, an extra burner and a new fridge. All this extra kit meant that we could let our creative juices flow and offer a larger menu. However, the only issue with all of this new kit was that we no longer had room to move around in our tiny shack. So we tracked down a guy to build us an extension. He also built us new work surfaces and a sink area comprised of an entire shelf under the counter for the slow cookers to sit on (we had amassed 10 by this stage); they were the workhorses of the breddos Tacos kitchen. Alongside the kit, we also realized that the local vegetable suppliers were not proving to be cost-effective, nor was their produce up to scratch. Thankfully, we lived pretty close to one of London's two giant wholesale fruit and vegetable markets. There was 'the avo guy', 'the herbs guy', several 'tomato guys', and once they got to know us, they started to set aside the best produce they had for when we came to visit early in the morning.

A few short months after we began trading, we had our first encounter with Jonathan Downey (aka JD), owner of the Rushmore Group and partner in Street Feast (now London Union), namely, a man who knew his stuff. Word had spread about our little shack and one morning in the middle of service we were mentioned in a tweet by JD saying that our tacos were his favourite in London. It's hard to describe how happy this made us. We had been speaking with JD for a couple of weeks when he invited us to compete in Taco Wars, the competition to find the UK's best taco. To say we were stoked would be an understatement! Taco Wars was a big deal for us and we wanted to make our mark. The decision was made to create the world's most complicated taco, so much so that it required one of us to stay up all night filling pipettes with hot sauce for one of the umpteen elements. The challenge was then for the three of us (one vegetarian girlfriend with a water bath full of short ribs, one breddo with RSI from pipette filling and the other with temporary anger management issues) to serve a hungry and discerning crowd of 550 people in a little over two hours. Added to this the shack was broken into two days before the event and someone made off with our over-aged short-ribs that we were going to braise down. What else could possibly go wrong?

Unsurprisingly, we didn't win. Surprisingly, we came second, but people seemed to love the craziness of that taco, affirming the path we were starting to take. By luck, one of the (many) components of these tacos was candied chillies, which required a lengthy cooking process; it began with boiling the chillies in a sweet vinegar solution for at least four hours, before then baking them for another two hours. Once the chillies were removed, the liquor left behind had taken on the heat and, in a simple happy accident, this, combined with the sharp, sweet character of the juice, created something delicious. Nud called over JD who tasted this nectar and immediately ran off to grab a bottle of tequila. After one shot of blanco tequila and a shot of the chilli juice we all decided that this was brilliant (after far too many shots); and the Chilliback was born...

It was at this early stage in our taco story that Street Feast began establishing itself as a cultural movement in London, creating some of the best food and drink experiences in derelict and disused spaces across the capital. We were invited to trade, firstly in the guest spot, then we slowly managed to establish ourselves as part of the core team. The people who attended Street Feast wanted to eat the world, which allowed us to truly push ourselves and develop our menus. As a platform for culinary experimentation and exposure to a great audience, we don't think there's anywhere more influential and important than Street Feast. It was revolutionizing the way Londoners ate and drank and really changed the game for us. Finally, part one of our dream was realized. We were able to quit our jobs and focus on breddos full time.

As we grew, we soon realized that our Golf GTi probably wasn't the best vehicle to be running a street food business out of. Yet we soldiered on, knowing that at some point we'd have to do something about it. That point came more quickly than we had envisaged... One day, JD called up and told us about a new project they had in mind called Truck Stop. The concept behind this was to amass loads of food trucks in Wood Wharf near Canary Wharf, which would sit alongside areas and bars created out of shipping containers. We were to be given pride of place next to the bar, a real coup for us. As always there was a snag; we had no truck... Despite hours spent searching, we were getting nowhere. Out of the blue, Nud bought a van on eBay. A 1984 VW LT31, which had a face like a Japanese animè fish. Work finished, we raced down to Surrey to inspect her and pick her up. Once we got there the scale of the thing was revealed – she was massive. Trying to appear like we knew what we were talking about, we looked at the mileage and kicked the tyres a bit. We were surprised to see that she'd only done 45,000 miles. This was brilliant, what a bargain! It was only later that we realized there were only five digits on the odometer and the true mileage was probably around 650,000... The princely sum of £1,300 was exchanged and she was ours. We christened her 'The Beast'. We sent her to a chap called Ockie in Cambridgeshire who transformed her into a food truck with hatches and hot water. Our friends at Jose Cuervo donated some money

to the cause and helped us design a motif that included our logo, Chilliback, Jose's logo and all manner of odd skull imagery. She was ready to go and looking fresh. Job done. This process, however, took a year, missing the deadline for Truck Stop by a solid nine months. Winning. It was only once all this work was done that we noticed we had neglected to include the word 'tacos' on the livery...

We returned to Taco Wars a year later. The competition was stiff this time. We settled upon a pimped-up version of our classic short-rib, with the addition of a few bits such as morello cherry jam to up the ante. Of course, this being Taco Wars, there was still a pipette involved, although this time around we didn't have to stay up all night filling the bloody things! Our secret weapon was giving away a Chilliback with every taco. We thought this was an ingenious idea, until almost half of our customers insisted that we join them in this libation. This time around, we won the competition. The best taco in the UK! We were over the moon but at the same time unable to string a sentence together due to the Chilliback debacle. Another day, another lesson learned...

Of course every journey begins with tentative first steps (and mis-steps) and over time we've grown and developed our culinary philosophy, celebrating the versatility of the humble taco. We should note that breddos Tacos is not an authentic Mexican offering. Although Nud spent a summer living there back in 2001, we are not Mexican. Our interpretation of the cuisine is based on a deep understanding of and huge respect for its history, and our approach has always been to take flavours, techniques and ingredients that we love from Mexico (and around the world) and develop recipes that we feel represent who we are, where we are from and where we are going.

The taco has always brought everything together on an edible plate. The space is limited to a 12cm (5 inch) diameter onto which we place our ingredients and we have always focused on sourcing the best ingredients we could find. This is the basis of the book you're currently reading. It's been an immensely fun and rewarding ride so far. We hope this comes across in our recipes and that you have as much fun creating them as we do.

## OUR RELATIONSHIP

### Nud on Chris

Chris and I met at university through our wider friendship group. Back then we had other things on our mind and to be honest, food was not one of them. We both moved to London from Manchester around the same time and shared a flat in Dalston. It was to be at least eight years until the idea of opening a food business dawned upon us.

Chris and I are very different beasts, with very different skill-sets. Whilst I manage the culinary and 'brand' related jobs, Chris looks after the finances and more importantly, the building of our sites. The latter is where Chris really excels – he has a very logical mind and craft skills to build our transient sites over a very short period of time. He also has the best handwriting in street food, although I still can't read most of it. Ultimately, as business partners, our skills complement each other rather than oppose or conflict and that is the key to our creative and operational output. I think we both agree that we're very lucky to have each other as partners and friends.

### Chris on Nud

The first thing that needs to be said and appreciated is that all of the recipes, and everything that we've ever done in terms of food, has come from Nud's head. I have never met anyone who thinks about food as much as he does!

We couldn't be any more different if we tried, but the fact that we both approach everything from different angles is one of the biggest strengths we have and I don't think either of us would change it. Although, sometimes we could kill each other. Most of the time, we're laughing and joking, but we're always trying to push things forward. It's a privilege working with such a talented guy, my best mate, my breddo.

# THE LARDER

*In this section you'll find most of the ingredients you'll need to make the recipes in this book. Although some of the ingredients may seem a bit obscure at first, once you begin to cook with them you'll quickly see the impact they make on dishes, adding saltiness, sweetness, sourness, umami, texture and pure chilli heat. Although we describe our food as non-traditional, we use Mexican ingredients extensively, so it's important to gain an understanding of these unusual ingredients and their uses. Some of them are more difficult to get hold of than others, so wherever possible, we'll offer an easy-to-get alternative or substitute. The best place to get hold of the harder-to-find ingredients is online through specific suppliers such as Mexgrocer.co.uk or Mexgrocer.com. However, some of the larger supermarkets are now starting to stock these more specific ingredients so it's worth checking their online stores.*

## CHILLIES | FRESH

### Jalapeño
A medium-sized chilli that has a mild to medium heat. They can be sourced through greengrocers but the medium green chillies (normally called 'serrano') which are available in packs from most supermarkets, will suffice.

### Birds-eye chillies
These little guys pack a punch that belies their size. At the lower end of the habanero heat scale but many times hotter than a jalapeño, we use them in our Asian-inspired dishes for an authentic Eastern heat. Easy to find in most greengrocers and supermarkets.

### Habanero/Scotch bonnets
Fresh habaneros are extremely hard to get hold of so we substitute these for Scotch bonnets, which are available from most greengrocers and supermarkets. They are close relations and although slightly sweeter, still have a powerful fruity citrus heat.

## CHILLIES | DRIED

### Cascabel chilli
These are also known as the rattle chilli due to the noise the seeds make within the hollow stomach of the chilli. They produce a great, mild and delicate flavour that works extremely well in salsas that require more depth of flavour than intensity of heat.

### Chipotle
Chipotles are smoke-dried, over-ripened jalapeños, give a mild heat and have a distinctive smoky flavour.

### Dried habanero
Like chipotles, these dried chillies are normally reserved for broths and slow cooking, where we tear them in for an intense heat. Unlike the chipotles they are not smoke-dried, retaining their fruity punch. (Back in the '90s these guys were classed as the hottest chillies in the world.)

### Guajillo
Large, medium-to-hot chillies that are generally used for broths but also in pastes and salsas. For salsas they are soaked, deseeded and deveined and ground into a paste.

### Ancho
Ancho is the name given to a dried poblano chilli and means 'wide' in Spanish. It is a large mild chilli that we use to give added depth to broths and salsas, alongside our ancho chilli oil (see page 134).

### Árbol chillies (chile de árbol)
Literally meaning 'tree chilli', these are smaller but very potent chillies. We tend to use them in their dry form to add to broths or infuse in oils. As they do have similar heat and taste characteristics to cayenne pepper, you can use it insead of these chillies.

## PASTES | HERBS | SPICES

### Achiote paste
Also known as recado rojo, this is a red paste made from a blend of spices with the ground seeds of the annatto plant. It's mainly used as an ingredient for marinades, most famously for the classic Cochinita Pibil.

### Cayenne pepper
A spicy powder derived from dried red chilli peppers, and a kitchen staple. Great for adding heat to broths and rubs.

### Smoked paprika
Another kitchen staple that's easy to get hold of. It's derived from dried red chillies and differs from regular paprika in that the farmers dry the chillies over large fires, which imparts a sweet smoky flavour to the powder.

### Ground cumin
Ground cumin seeds were brought into Mexican cuisine by the Spanish many years ago. It adds an earthy, warm taste. Like most of the herbs and spices we use, this is readily available from your local supermarket.

### Tinned tomatillos
Tomatillos or Mexican husked tomatoes are a key ingredient in fresh green salsas. A close relative of the Cape gooseberry, they are available fresh but tend to be expensive, so it's best to use the tinned variety.

### Chipotle chilli powder
This adds a wonderful smoky flavour to marinades. Of course, if you're having trouble getting hold of this powder and you have dried chipotles, you can blitz them for the same effect.

### Chipotle in adobo
A key ingredient in our chipotle ketchup, these are plump chipotles in a delicious, smoky adobo sauce.

### Mexican oregano
You may be forgiven for thinking that this is simply 'normal' oregano but it's actually an entirely different plant, with a grassy taste and citrus note. It can be purchased through specialist suppliers but if you're stuck you can try using dried marjoram, which has similar floral notes.

### Epazote
This is a Mexican herb that has a very pungent smell and taste, think aniseed and fennel, only stronger. Its aroma has been compared to petroleum!

### Star anise
A Chinese spice that we use to enhance the flavours of our meat, particularly beef. Readily available from supermarkets.

### Allspice
This is the dried unripe berries of the pimenta tree ground into a powder. Mainly grown in the Caribbean, its name was coined by the English who thought it combined the flavours of cinnamon, nutmeg and cloves.

## OTHER INGREDIENTS

### Onion powder
Dehydrated and ground onion.

### Garlic powder
Dehydrated and ground garlic.

### Salt
We always use good quality sea salt flakes such as Maldon sea salt.

### Dijon mustard
We use this as an ingredient in mayonnaise and aïoli.

### Fish sauce
An Asian staple, this comes from fermenting anchovies in water and salt. We use this intense flavour mainly in our Asian-influenced recipes.

### Dark soy sauce
One of the oldest condiments in the world and a kitchen staple. We tend to use dark soy as it's less salty than light soy. Perfect for adding umami to dishes.

### Vinegars
We use various vinegars for a wide range of uses; aïolis and mayonnaise, pickling and adding acidity. The vinegars we use regularly: red wine vinegar, white wine vinegar, cider vinegar, sherry vinegar and muscatel vinegar.

## ESSENTIAL EQUIPMENT

### Cast iron/ovenproof frying pan or griddle pan
A lot of our cooking involves roasting, braising and grilling. It's always helpful to be able to start a dish off on the hob (cooktop) and finish it in the oven, thus freeing up the hob to cook the other elements of dishes.

### Blender
If there's one thing you need more than anything to cook our food, it's a blender. Most of our dishes involve some kind of paste, marinade or a blend of spices. Traditionally Mexicans would use a molcajete, a granite pestle and mortar, but for speed and efficiency, the blender is a winner.

### Pestle and mortar
Essential to grind toasted spices and make salsas the traditional way.

### Slow cooker
We'd highly recommend you buy one for your home kitchen. They make cooking meat over a long period of time much easier.

### Tortilla press
Very useful if you want to make your own tortillas.

## WHAT IS A...

### Taco
The thing you've been waiting all day to eat! This is the base, the meat, the salsa, the whole shebang.

### Tortilla
This is what we call the edible plate. Traditionally made from dried corn that has been nixtamalized and turned into a dough called masa, which is then cooked to make a tortilla. We make our tortillas from masa harina (see page 16) and they measure between 12-15cm (5–6 inches). If you don't make them, corn tortillas are widely available at supermarkets and local bodegas in similar sizes.

### Tostada
Take a tortilla and deep fry it until it's crunchy.

## RYE TORTILLAS

### INGREDIENTS

**Makes 25 tortillas (around 12–15cm/5–6 inch)**

300ml (10½oz/1⅓ cups) warm water
1 level teaspoon yeast
500g (17½oz/3¼ cups) organic rye flour
2 teaspoons salt
1 tablespoon rapeseed oil
1 teaspoon sesame seeds (optional)

1. Mix the warm water with the yeast and stir. Leave until bubbles form. Then add the rye flour, salt, oil and seeds, if using, and combine to form a dough. Knead for 4 minutes, cover with a kitchen (dish) towel and leave for 1 hour in a warm place.

2. Follow the tortilla making process (see page 16). Repeat with the rest of the dough.

3. Cook in a hot cast-iron pan for 2 minutes on each side, or until the tortilla is slightly crunchy but still malleable.

## DONG'S FLATBREADS

*Dong has worked for us for two years now and came in all shy and quiet. Like most shy and quiet people, he has a sparkling personality. He is also an incredible young chef. Out of the blue one day, he made these astonishing flatbreads. We normally barbecue them over coals, but you can also cook them in a frying pan or an oven.*

### INGREDIENTS

**Makes 10-15 flatbreads (around 30cm/12 inch)**

3 level teaspoons dried yeast
600ml (21fl oz/2¾ cups) warm water
1kg (35oz/7½ cups) plain (all-purpose) flour
2 tablespoons sea salt
5 tablespoons natural yoghurt
rapeseed or garlic oil

1. Put the yeast into a bowl with the warm water and stir to dissolve, then add the flour and mix to a dough. Leave to rest for 30 minutes, then add the salt and yoghurt. Knead until incorporated, about 4–5 minutes. Leave the dough to rest in a warm place for 45 minutes. Knead again for 4–5 minutes, then set aside for 2 hours for the final rest.

2. Divide the dough into equal portions and roll out to a 5mm (¼ inch) thickness. Heat a cast-iron pan or griddle to high, add a slick of rapeseed or garlic oil and cook the breads one at a time for about 2 minutes each side.

## CORN TORTILLAS

*A taco press makes life much simpler. You can use shop-bought corn tortillas for our recipes if you don't fancy making your own.*

## INGREDIENTS

**Makes 25 tortillas (around 12–15cm/5-6 inch)**

160g (5½oz/scant 1¼ cups) masa harina (or blue masa
   harina for blue tortillas)
½ teaspoon salt
100ml (3½fl oz/scant ½ cup) hot water
1 tablespoon rapeseed oil or melted lard

1. Mix the masa harina and salt in a bowl and stir in the water slowly whilst mixing the dough with your hand. Add the oil and knead to form a smooth dough. If the dough is too wet, add some more masa harina and if it feels flaky and dry, add some more water. Leave to rest at room temperature for a minimum of 30 minutes.

2. Divide the dough into 25 equal-sized balls.

3. Cut a freezer bag in half to create two square sections and place onto a hard surface or on the bottom of your tortilla press. Add a ball of masa then place the other freezer bag square over the top of the dough. Either push your hand down firmly on the dough or use a rolling pin to create a 12-15cm (5-6 inch) circular tortilla, or if you are using a taco press, press down using the crank lever. Remove the plastic squares and set the tortilla aside. Repeat, separating each pressed tortilla with a square of baking (parchment) paper.

5. Heat a heavy-based pan and add the tortillas – cook 1 minute on each side, or until they soufflé slightly. Remove after a minute or 2 and wrap in a tea (dish) towel to keep warm.

BEEF

## PORTER BRAISED BEEF SHORT-RIB & BURNT SPRING ONION CREMA

1. Sprinkle the short-ribs with the salt and set aside for 2 hours.

2. Heat 1 tablespoon of the oil in a frying pan on a medium heat and add the short ribs. You want to sear the ribs on all sides and get a deep-brown, caramel colour on them. Don't skip this step, as it's imperative for building the umami flavour. When browned, remove from the heat.

3. In an ovenproof casserole, heat the remaining tablespoon of oil on a medium heat and add the onion and leek. Cook for 5 minutes, then add the garlic. After 3 minutes, add the soy sauce, ketchup, brown sugar, anise, cayenne pepper, chile de árbol, chipotles, mushrooms and beer. Cook the mixture for 30 minutes, uncovered, on a low heat, then add the short ribs to the pot. If there seems to be too little liquid to cover the ribs, add some water.

4. Preheat your oven to 130°C (250°F/Gas ½). Once it's up to temperature, cover the casserole with a lid then transfer to the oven and cook for 6–8 hours. The short-ribs are ready when you can scoop some meat off them with a teaspoon. Remove from the oven and, when cool, take the ribs out and put them on a tray. Put the casserole back on a medium heat and reduce the sauce for another 20 minutes or so – this will be your glaze, so you're looking for a sauce that will thickly coat the back of a spoon.

5. When you're ready to eat, heat a frying pan over a medium heat and add the ribs, rib side down. Using a brush, glaze the ribs with the reduced sauce, then flip them and cook them meat side down for 5 minutes. Turn and brush again.

6. Warm the tortillas in a dry pan. Place two on each plate and cover the tacos with a thin layer of the burnt spring onion crema. Pull the meat away from the bone of each rib, using a fork and spoon, and place on the tacos. Sprinkle the coriander over, followed by some chilli flakes. Serve with the lime and pico de gallo on the side.

## INGREDIENTS

**SERVES 4**

2kg (4½lb) beef short-ribs
1½ tablespoons sea salt
2 tablespoons olive oil
1 onion, finely chopped
1 leek, roughly chopped
7 garlic cloves, finely chopped
70ml (2½fl oz/scant ⅓ cup) soy sauce
70ml (2½fl oz/scant ⅓ cup) ketchup
130g (4½oz/½ cup) brown sugar
3 star anise
1 tablespoon cayenne pepper
2 tablespoons chile de árbol powder
4 dried chipotle chillies
5 dried porcini mushrooms
1 x 440ml (15fl oz/scant 2 cups) can of porter, or other dark beer

**To serve:**
8 corn tortillas (see page 16)
100ml (3½fl oz/scant ½ cup) burnt spring onion (scallions) crema (see page 138)
4 tablespoons chopped coriander (cilantro)
chilli flakes, to serve
2 limes, quartered
4 tablespoons pico de gallo (see page 132)

# JALAPEÑO CHEESEBURGER

*Everyone loves a good burger, and when breddos Tacos
were asked to take over the kitchen at a basement cocktail
bar in Soho, part of the remit was for us to design a small
burger menu to complement our tacos. With Chris loving
burgers more than life itself and being a true connoisseur
of the meat sandwich, our task was to create a burger that
would first and foremost please him.*

*Ask your butcher to grind the mince coarsely for you –
this will give a loose, crumbly texture. You'll need a lid
of some kind for your frying pan to achieve superior
melted cheese. I highly recommend cooking your
burger to medium rare, which means you want to take
the burger off the heat when the meat's internal
temperature reaches 55°C (130°F).*

1. Separate the mince into four 150g (5½oz) balls.

2. Split your brioche buns and toast until slightly brown.
Squirt some ketchup and chipotle mayonnaise on the base
of the bun then add some lettuce and gherkins.

3. Heat a thick-based cast-iron frying pan or griddle until
smoking hot and add the mince balls, pressing them down
with your hand or a spatula from the top to create a thick
2–3cm (¾–1 inch) patty. Season the raw side of the patties
with a big pinch of the salt and pepper mix. Add the
jalapeños and the shallot to the pan with the butter and
cook for 7 minutes until soft and caramelized and a nice
crust has formed on the cooked side of the patties, then
flip them and season the cooked side.

4. Top each patty with 2 cheese slices, some of the
cooked jalapeños and a few of the shallots, then add the
water to the frying pan or griddle, immediately putting the
lid on to contain all the steam. After a minute, take the
lid off the frying pan and add the tops of the buns to the
burgers. Add another splash of water and put the lid back
on. Cook for 45 seconds, then take the burgers out of the
pan and put them on to their brioche bases.

## INGREDIENTS

**SERVES 4**

600g (1lb 5oz) dry-aged, coarsely ground beef chuck
and short-rib (25% fat content)

4 brioche rolls, preferably not too sweet

4 teaspoons ketchup, or to taste

4 teaspoons chipotle mayonnaise (see page 138)

½ head of lettuce, leaves shredded

1 gherkin, sliced into thick rounds

1 tablespoon sea salt mixed with 1 tablespoon freshly
ground black pepper

2 jalapeño chillies, thinly sliced into rings

1 shallot, finely diced

1 tablespoon butter

8 slices American processed cheese

25ml (1fl oz/2 tablespoons) water

# NE ASADA & CHIPOTLE CASHEW SALSA

*s my take on a classic Mexican street food taco.*
*ughout Mexico, these vary in both recipe and*
*entation, so I thought we'd do the same with our*
*dos Tacos version. I use the chipotle cashew nut salsa*
*d a creamy, nutty and smoky flavour to the taco.*
*ts would definitely frown at our treatment of the*
*e asada, but the taste combination speaks for itself.*

o the smoky steak marinade all over the steak and
the meat to marinate in the refrigerator, covered, for
st an hour and up to 2 days.

hen you're ready, get the grill or pan as hot as you
about 5 minutes on a high heat, then add the steak
cook until it's charred on the outside and medium
on the inside, about 3 minutes on each side. Take
teak off the grill and let it rest for 5 minutes in a
place. In the meantime, warm up the tortillas in
frying pan and wrap them in a clean tea (dish) towel
ep them warm.

ce the steak against the grain into 2cm (¾ inch) thick
s. Put a few slices of steak on each tortilla, add some
ew nut salsa, some pico de gallo, a squirt of lime, a
nful of sour cream or crema, and some coriander
rnish.

## INGREDIENTS

**SERVES 4**

500g (1lb 2oz) bavette, onglet steak or rump

**For the marinade:**
300ml (11fl oz/1¼ cups) smoky steak marinade
  (see page 139)

**To serve:**
16 corn tortillas (see page 16)
4 tablespoons chipotle cashew nut salsa (see page 134)
4 tablespoons pico de gallo (see page 132)
2 limes, quartered
100ml (3½fl oz/scant ½ cup) sour cream or crema
  (see page 140)
a handful of coriander leaves (cilantro)

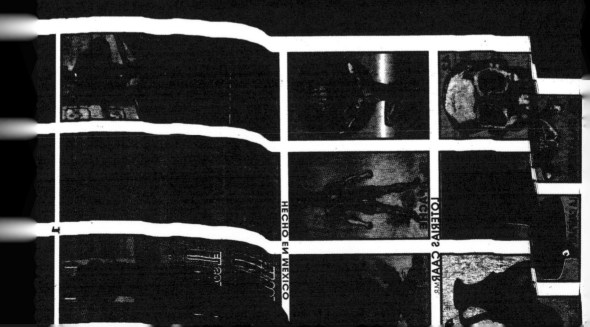

## BEEF TARTARE, TOMATILLO & JALAPEÑO

1. Put the beef fillet into the freezer to firm up for 30 minutes. Very finely dice the shallot and leave to soak in a bowl of cold water while the beef is in the freezer.

2. Finely dice the cornichons, red chilli, jalapeño, and finely chop the tomatillo and crispy garlic and put them into a bowl with the drained shallots. Slice the beef fillet and cut into 5mm (¼ inch) cubes, add to the bowl with the teaspoon of the olive oil and mix together.

3. Add the red wine vinegar, a pinch of salt, and a bigger pinch of pepper, the mustard and extra-virgin olive oil and mix. Place a tostada (or 2) on each plate and add a spoonful of tartare mix. Spread out to cover the surface. Place a raw egg yolk in the middle and sprinkle with salt and pepper.

4. Garnish with coriander, radish slices and breddos hot sauce, and finish with edible flowers, if using.

## INGREDIENTS

**SERVES 4 AS A SNACK | 2 AS A MAIN COURSE**

150g (5½oz) good quality beef fillet
1 shallot
3 cornichons
1 long red chilli
1 jalapeño chilli
1 tomatillo, dry roasted
1 garlic clove, sliced wafer thin and sautéd in olive oil
 until crispy
1 teaspoon olive oil
1 tablespoon red wine vinegar
sea salt and freshly ground black pepper
1 teaspoon Dijon mustard
2 tablespoons extra-virgin olive oil
4 tostada (see page 14)
4 quail egg yolks
4 tablespoons finely chopped coriander (cilantro),
 to garnish
thinly sliced radishes, to garnish
1 tablespoon breddos hot sauce (see page 132)
 or to taste
edible flowers (optional), to garnish

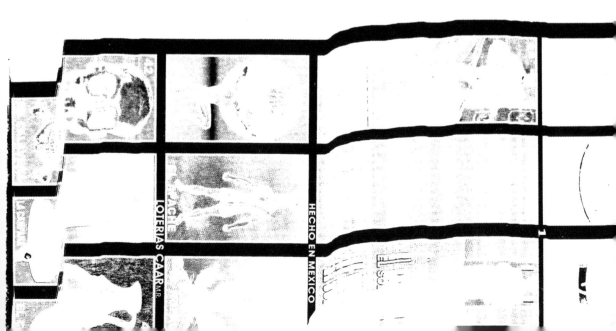

# BONE-IN RIB-EYE, TOMATOES, BURNT SPRING ONIONS & SHACK SALSA

*I cooked this on a drum barbecue in a tiny shack over on the rooftop of Street Feast Dinerama in Shoreditch, London, in the middle of summer.*

*Ask your butcher for bone-in rib-eye steaks that have been dry-aged for at least 28 days. The steak will taste best when cooked over charcoal, but a heavy-based frying pan and intense heat will do the trick. Be sure to take the steaks out of the refrigerator at least an hour before you intend on cooking them, so they are at room temperature.*

## INGREDIENTS

### SERVES 4

2 x 400g (14oz) bone-in
    rib-eye steaks
3 tablespoons butter
4 garlic cloves, peeled
1 sprig of thyme
sea salt and freshly ground
    black pepper
100ml (3½fl oz/scant ½
    cup) red wine
4 large Datterini tomatoes,
    or any very sweet
    tomatoes

extra-virgin olive oil
1 red onion, finely sliced
    into rings and soaked in
    cold water
thyme oil (see page 134)
1 tablespoon ancho chilli
    oil (see page 134)
5 tablespoons shack salsa
    verde (see page 135)
a handful of coriander
    (cilantro), chopped
1 teaspoon ground red
    chilli powder
a bunch of burnt spring
    onions (see page 138)
10 corn tortillas
    (see page 16)

1. When you're ready to cook, turn your hob to high and place your frying pan or griddle on to get it seriously hot (leave it for at least 5 minutes). Pat dry the steaks (this is important so that the steaks char rather than steam) and put them into the pan. Keep them moving around in the pan and after 3–4 minutes, flip them over.

2. Add 1 tablespoon of the butter to the pan and baste the steak with the rendered fat and melted butter. Add the garlic and thyme. Add a big pinch of the sea salt and pepper to the side of the rib-eye that's been cooking, cook for a further 4 minutes (for medium rare), then

transfer the steaks to a warm plate. Add ½ tablespoon of butter on top of each steak and leave to rest for at least 5 minutes.

3. Add the red wine to the pan with the remaining tablespoon of butter. Turn up the heat and let the sauce reduce for 5 minutes, then set aside.

4. Cut the tomatoes into 1cm (½ inch) slices, then drizzle on some olive oil and sprinkle with sea salt and pepper. Place the sliced tomatoes on a serving plate and add the drained red onions. Slice the steak across the grain at a 45-degree angle into 3cm (1¼ inch) segments and place on top of the tomatoes. Drizzle with a little thyme oil, the ancho chilli oil, 2 tablespoons of salsa verde, and sprinkle with the coriander, red chilli and some sea salt. Place the burnt spring onions on the side.

5. Warm the tortillas in a dry frying pan then serve, with each guest grabbing a couple of slices of steak and some tomatoes and onions. If you like it hot, have some habanero hot sauce on the side.

## LENGUA WITH PUMPKIN SEED SALSA

*People are often scared of eating offal, but in Mexico
and other parts of the world it is celebrated for its texture,
flavour and value. Tongue is widely available in Mexico and
is incredibly easy to cook with as long as you don't mind
a bit of peeling! The texture is great and works really well
with the crunch from the pumpkin and sesame seeds in
the salsa.*

1. Wash the tongues under cold water, to make sure they
are clean. Put them into a deep stockpot and add the
rest of the ingredients except for the olive oil. Cover with
water, then cover the pot and place on a medium heat
for 3–4 hours. The tongues are ready when a paring knife
easily cuts through the skin.

2. Remove the tongues from the braising liquid and leave
to cool. When they are cool, take a small paring knife and
peel the skin off. Discard the skin and slice each tongue
lengthways into strips.

3. When you're ready to eat, heat a frying pan with a
slick of oil and add the tongue slices – you're looking
to get some caramelization on the outside, so have
the heat high and keep the cooking time short, 2 or 3
minutes maximum.

4. Warm up your tortillas in a dry frying pan, then fill with
the tongue, salsas and coriander and serve with the limes.

## INGREDIENTS

**SERVES 4**

**For the tongue:**
2 ox tongues
2 bay leaves
4 tablespoons black peppercorns
2 onions, quartered
1 carrot, roughly chopped
1 guajillo chilli
1 ancho chilli
1 bouquet garni (thyme, oregano and rosemary)
2 tablespoons sea salt
olive oil, for frying

**To serve:**
12 corn tortillas (see page 16)
4 tablespoons sesame seed & pumpkin seed salsa
(see page 137)
salsa roja (see page 136), to taste
a handful of coriander (cilantro)
2 limes, quartered

# TACO
# TRAIL

# THE FIRST TRIP: NYC, LA, DF

## The cities: NYC, LA and Mexico

We decided that our first trip would consist of spending four or five days in three cities that were creating the greatest things in the name of the taco. We embarked on an impressive amount of research and came up with a terrifyingly long list of where we had to eat over the course of the trip. To get through our list, we worked out that we were going to be averaging 10 spots a day. Still we soldiered on, risking our own health, souls, relationships and potentially a nasty case of gout, all for the greater good.

## First stop was NYC

A very good friend of ours picked us up from the airport for a catch-up lunch at her house in New Jersey before we travelled into Manhattan. Although we had mentioned our insane eating schedule to our hosts, after half an hour Nat's husband James shouted that lunch was served and out came a 10oz porterhouse steak with the full works. This pretty much set the tone for the rest of the trip.

Feeling enormously full and not a little bit tipsy, we jumped (or rather lugged ourselves) on the train to Manhattan. The hotel we were staying at was The Jane, located on the edge of the meat-packing district. Our room was so small that we had to take it in turns to get ready, with one person standing in the hotel corridor outside. From this point onwards, we decided not to spend much time in the room, for both of our sanities.

To kick off, our first dinner was at The Black Ant on the Lower East Side. We had been keen to try this place for ages as they were known for having developed an entirely modern take on Mexican food. We then went on to having a couple more suppers before calling it a night.

The next few days passed by in a bit of a gluttonous blur. By day we would hit up all the taco joints like Choza in Gotham West, Tacos No. 1 in West Chelsea and markets such as the newly opened Gansevoort Market in the meat-packing district. At each place we visited we would order the majority of the menu; this involved a hell of a LOT of braised meat. By night we would hit up the restaurants and the bars: Danny Bowien's Mission Cantina, Alex Stupak's Empellón and Empellón Cocina. In terms of bars, Attaboy on the Lower East Side, formerly Milk and Honey, was a knockout. It was at this point that our time in New York started to get a little hazy in the way that only New York can. The whole city is so compact and incredibly intense, and our hotel room only compounded both of these senses.

## California, California

It was time to get on a plane and head west to California. Neither of us had been there, but we were armed from a local guy with the next cracking list of where to eat. We landed at LAX and hired a car, a convertible Mustang obviously (and not as some would have it, a hairdresser's car). The first thing that struck us about LA, was its sheer size. It was absolutely massive. Not just in geographical terms –as even its roads were vast and everything was low rise and sprawling. It was the antithesis of New York.

The next day, we woke up early. There were some serious tacos to discover after all. We jumped into the car, put the roof down and headed out to pursue tacos anew, and felt the first licks of the Californian sun tickle our skin. First stop was Guisados in east LA. N.B. At this point we should mention that after four days of eating non-stop tacos, something happens to a man. Your physiology starts to change, it's as if your body starts to sense the potential fat content in the air, and if you walk past braising meat, you have a physical reaction. Which is pretty much your body rejecting what's about to be put in it. We arrived at Guisados and as soon as we opened the door we were hit with that smell. Braised meat. It was at this point that our knees started to knock and we both wanted to cry. Against our instincts and our bodies' wishes, we entered.

We got chatting to the owner. We explained what we were doing in the US and he insisted we try... everything. It was just 10a.m. After eating all his fantastic tacos, he took us next door to his brother's shop where they nixtamalized all of the corn for the tortillas in-house. He explained that 'guisado' meant 'braised'. Duh! This became one of the more useful bits of knowledge that we learnt on the whole trip...

The level of eating continued apace. We would drive for 20 minutes then stop for some tacos, drive, tacos, drive, tacos... The evening of the second day arrived and the main event, dinner at Animal. This was one of the restaurants we were most looking forward to and it did not disappoint; once we had found it, that is. There's no name on the door. The menu was vast and it's one of those rare places where you could eat every single thing on it. Dish after dish of amazing-ness arrived and was duly demolished. Whilst we were eating we noticed a bar across the road that also had no name on the door, it just had a couple of burly looking chaps outside. We asked a newly acquired friend what the deal was and he explained that it was called 'No name' and was, at that moment LA's hottest bar. We queried as to our chances of getting in, 'You can try' was the response. So, of course, we walked across the road where Nud put on his poshest accent and explained we were from out of town. The guy disappeared inside, a few minutes later he came out and ushered us in. From here on in things got a bit blurry. We vaguely remember being stood next to Justin Timberlake, boring one of the guys from Tame Impala to death and having an in-depth chat on feminism with his friend, a very pretty lead singer from a band whose name escaped us. Apparently we went to Soho House at some point that night. We definitely went to one club where the girls were so pretty we had to leave. At some point we had an almighty argument somewhere on Sunset Strip and went our separate ways.

We both woke up in the morning feeling more than a little sheepish. Still we had a mission to complete. So we loaded ourselves back into the car and headed to find a place simply called 'the best fish tacos in Ensenada'. The last thing either of us wanted to do was to go and eat tacos, but this was our MO, our raison d'être; the entire reason why we were here, so we proceeded to order two of everything on offer. Taking the first bite with trepidation, what occurred was entirely unexpected. They were a revelation! So simple, just fish battered and fried in a massive wok right in front of you, seasoned to perfection with a choice of salsas. It was so good we ordered more.

We jumped back into the car and drove back down the hill, and about 200 yards down the road we saw a truck, Ricky's Tacos parked on the side of the road. This was also on our hit list so we stopped and ordered more fish tacos. Fantastic again. We were getting into our stride now. Next stop was downtown to the arts district. We arrived at Grand Central Market, filled with authentic Mexican stands selling both produce and the finished articles: tacos, quesadillas, enchiladas. There were stands selling moles, all manner of chillies, fresh and dried tortillas. This place brought home how seriously California, and indeed the US in general, takes its Mexican food.

We then decided to check out Guerrilla Tacos, a truck doing really interesting things with their food, exactly what we had come here to eat. It was brilliant and chef Wes Avila's twist on classic Mexican fare was really inspiring. However, at this point, we had started hallucinating from too many calories and urgently needed a respite from our eating agenda. Nothing fancy, stay in, pizza, movie, refreshed and ready to go the next day. At about 11.30p.m. Nud burst into action.

"Right, c'mon, we've got to go."

"What?!" I replied.

"Kogi, they're gonna be at such and such place in 30 minutes. C'mon, sort yourself out."

However much we didn't want to go, and we really didn't, these were the guys that started everything. The original food truck that kicked everything off. Roy Choi is a demi-god in the LA and global food scene and has a fleet of trucks that tweet where they are going. To go to LA and not seek them out, given what we do, would have been crazy. We fired the street name into the sat nav and sped off. We arrived at a nondescript corner and parked up. No sign of the truck. Moments later, the famous truck rolled into view, instantly recognizable. What seemed like five seconds later an enormous queue appeared snaking off into the distance. Where the hell had everyone come from? Thankfully, we were at the front of the queue. The famous Korean short-rib tacos, black jack quesadillas... the works. The guy at the front was the man himself, Roy bloody Choi! We were so full that we could only manage a few bites of each taco but it was enough to confirm that the hype was totally justified.

Strangely, when we woke up, breakfast wasn't the first thing on our minds. Besides, we had a brunch date with Chris, the illusive dude who had supplied tips for our hit list, at a restaurant that we'd never heard of, but had insisted was unmissable. So, we headed south east towards Corazón y Miel, which turned out to be in a Latino neighbourhood that had a massive Mexican hypermarket that sold absolutely everything in the world.

We wandered round agog at its size before Nud got us booted out for filming a shelf full of tortillas. We headed over the road and in through another unnamed door into a restaurant that was buzzing. We'd never met Chris before, as we had communicated solely through email, so it was a real pleasure to meet the guy who'd helped us out with so many recommendations for the trip. It turned out that Chris worked in the movie business and that he was currently working on a project that was particularly close to his heart, the premise of the show was to follow individual chefs who were doing particularly brilliant things and to showcase their journey.

We woke up on our final morning, to yet another perfect, sunshine-filled LA day. We had a few hours to kill before we jumped on another plane that would take us to Mexico City, so we drove up to the Griffith Observatory to have a look at the spectacular views.

What. A. City.

### Next stop, DF Mexico
As we flew over Mexico City, we couldn't get over the sheer scale of the place. This was in a completely different league, even to LA. We flew over the city for half an hour before we landed.

Upon arrival, we hopped in a cab and headed over to the apartment we had rented, situated in La Condesa, one of the cooler neighbourhoods and the home to many of the restaurants we had on our list. We had done a ton of research and curated a formidable list of restaurants, stalls and markets that we needed to visit. Due to our relatively relaxed last few days in LA, a kind of complacency had set in. This was about to be shattered into a million tiny pieces over the next few days...

The first morning was spent navigating the maze that is La Condessa, stopping at every taquería we could find and ordering the whole menu. This really was a beautiful neighbourhood with tree-lined streets, small parks in the middle of islands and squares boasting amazing architecture. The vast majority of the tacos in DF are very traditional; guisado or chorizo garnished with onions and a touch of coriander (cilantro) with a choice of salsas (normally three). DF is also the home of tacos al pastor. If you've not come across these, they're tacos that are cut from a large mass of marinated pork shoulder cutlets piled on top of one another on a revolving *trompo* (picture a chicken doner). On the top of the spit is a whole pineapple and when all the meat is shaved into your taco, the taquero cuts and flicks a chunk of pineapple on top. Their dexterity is utterly impressive; they could probably flick a piece into a beer bottle on a table 10 feet away. Its origins come from Lebanese settlers who combined their native techniques with the established way of doing things in Mexico.

We then decided to head out to the bars that lined the streets of La Roma. We turned into a massive road and lo and behold there were bars and restaurants everywhere;

some of which looked much more salubrious than others. We spent an evening getting to know the bars and taquerías of La Roma. There were fantastic drinks, including the best margarita either of us had ever had, in a lovely bar that we completely forgot to get the name of (handy eh?). We decided to call it a night. On our way back (slightly worse for wear) we walked past a doorway with lots of people standing outside, alongside a couple of intimidating bouncers. The doorway was nothing special, a simple light leading to an old wooden staircase. Given the clientele, this place warranted further inspection. After confirming that it was indeed a bar (always a good idea), we climbed up the winding staircase and what greeted us at the top was staggering. Between two higher buildings they'd built a conservatory that was about 40 feet high, with sliding glass panels that opened the place up to the heavens. There were massive palm trees around the dimly lit room where all of DF's bright young things sat. It was a thing to behold. You couldn't help but be seduced by everything about it. It turned out that this place was called Romita Comedor. We managed to work this out after about an hour of staring at a 20-foot (6 metres) neon sign only 6 feet (1.8 metres) from where we sitting with the bar's name emblazoned on it. It was time to go.

The next day we decided to hit the markets. We headed towards the biggest of them all, La Merced. The size of the markets was absolutely staggering. You could wander around for half an hour and you wouldn't even have got through the crisp section. Piles and piles of cleanly prepped vegetables sat stacked up in perfect symmetry and order. We could easily have lost a day in the place. One of the other benefits is the market is also rammed full of mini-food courts, so you're never more than a hundred yards from a taco. By the time it came to lunch, there was a place that Nud wanted to check out called Contramar, located in La Condesa. The place was humming with people and waiters alike. As luck would have it, one of the highly coveted outside tables became available just as we were at the front of the queue, a perfect place to watch the great and good flow in and out of the restaurant. Despite initially having to force ourselves to open our mouths, we managed to demolish a fair few of their star turns.

That night we had the main event: Pujol, which was regarded as the most forward-thinking Mexican restaurant in the world. We were quite literally chomping at the bit to see what the chef, Enrique Olvera had got. Upon sitting down, we were whisked through course after course of food pushing boundary after boundary. The smoked ant was superb as were the signature new and old moles. One mole was freshly made, the other was just over a year old and was fed every day so it continually gained richness and intensity.

The next day we had the pleasure of being shown around the city by Maurizio and his girlfriend Franci, who were both locals. Maurizio, an artist, had grown up in DF and had returned after living all over the world. The first place they took us to was an old cantina next to a massive park, a true vision of old school Mexico. We had to sit area as women were not allowed in the main restaurant. (Like we said, old school.) We then continued bopping round from place to place, enjoying the lack of responsibility that comes with being shown around. Cafés, bars, taquerías; all were taken in on this whistle-stop tour. As late afternoon turned into an early dusk-filled hazy evening, Maurizio decided to take us for the perfect margarita. It was a trek, he explained, but well worth it and something he used to do with his family. Perfect margarita? He didn't get any complaints from us. After an hour in the cab we started to notice the houses around us getting bigger and bigger and disappearing behind more and more giant gates with bodyguards outside.

Upon arrival, we piled out of our battered little cab and walked through the entrance into a garden that would make the Beverly Hills Country Club look cheap. This was without a doubt the smartest place we had ever been to. We went to sit in a garden filled with candles and lanterns and Maurizio ordered four margaritas. They brought out frozen glasses with limes, along with miniature silver wine buckets, full of ice, on top of which sat a silver flask containing the hallowed margarita. All of this pomp and splendour certainly added to the experience.

When it reached dinnertime we headed back to La Roma and Maurizio's favourite restaurant, run by a friend of his who incidentally used to work at Pujol. We entered Máximo Bistrot and were greeted like old friends. It was a cute little place, with a very low key and buzzy vibe. This turned out to be one of the best meals of the trip, sensational food and atmosphere and a brilliant way to round off our epic trip.

---------------------------------------------------------------------

During the summer of 2015, we were approached by the folks at Quadrille Publishing, who asked if we'd like to write a book. The one that you're reading now, as it happens. "Us? What? Really?" was what initially sprung to mind.

We had a lot on at that point planning the route we wanted breddos Tacos to take, and the thought of writing a book was daunting to say the least. How do we even start? How do we fill it?

"If we're doing a book, mate, we need to go on another trip." said Nud.

"Well then, let's do the book." I said.

# TRIP NO. 2: THE SECOND TACO COMING

This time around we wanted to check out the places that were doing the most inventive things with, yes you guessed it, tacos. Top of the list was Baja California and in particular Ensenada and the Valle de Guadeloupe, the Mexican wine country. Next on the list was San Francisco. A place that had been seared into our memories by virtue of Hollywood and somewhere neither of us had been to before but were both itching to go to; however contentious that would be with our girlfriends... Finally, and fortuitously, we were going to go back to LA. Too great a city, too good an opportunity to miss...

## San Fran

We arrived in downtown San Francisco, all hustle and bustle and a hell of a lot warmer than we had expected. First place on this trip list was State Bird Provisions. Everyone that we knew or had ever met raved about this place, so we had to go and chance the massive queue that was apparently a permanent fixture. We turned up expecting to see the infamous line snaking down the road. Nothing. By sheer fluke we'd managed to time it perfectly and we just strolled on in. The method of serving was unlike anywhere else we had experienced. You got your menu, ordered the dishes you wanted and trolleys would come round with small plates that you could add to your meal. Being completely unaccustomed to this style of dining, we went in hard, taking a small plate from the trolley nearly every time one was offered to us. By the time the food we ordered arrived, we were absolutely stuffed. Everything we ate was delicious, not a dud note to be found, from the Kung Pao beef tongue to the deep fried garlic bread filled with burrata. Full to the brim, the only thing for it was to go and find some bars and see what the nightlife of this famous city had to offer. Being the first night we got a little bit too excited and what ensued was another one of those lost evenings. Suffice to say we managed to try the entire list at a bar whose name still escapes us and we both recall spending some time in a bar that resembled a pirate ship.

The next few days were spent wandering around the Mission district, trying all of the taco joints that were recommended to us. If we're completely honest, nothing really stood out and captured our imagination – in terms of authenticity, the tacos were great, but we were hungry for more. We were looking for food that was changing the game.

Our best evening in San Fran started at Al's Place, voted by Bon Appetit as USA's best restaurant in 2015. The flavours that chef Aaron London created, coupled with the presentation and stark white dining room, created a truly unforgettable meal.

That was it for San Francisco. Maybe we did it wrong, maybe there were other spots that we missed that would have blown us away. One thing's for sure, San Francisco, great city that it was, really didn't suck us in and beguile us like LA had done the year before. Speaking of which, it was time to head back to the city of angels...

LA take II

We picked up a car (another convertible Mustang, naturally) and headed to our usual hotel in West Hollywood. On this trip we were actually going to be in LA twice, three days on this stint and then back again for a couple of nights after Baja and before our return to London. This afforded us the luxury of not having to go too bonkers. We could revisit some of our favourite haunts from the last trip and check out any newcomers that fell into our new remit. Bliss.

Over the course of the next few days we went back to Animal (just as brilliant), best fish tacos in Ensenada (good but not as good as we had remembered) and Guerrilla Tacos (awesome as always). There were new places that we tried like Jonny and Vinny's, a pizza place from the guys that own Animal and Son of a Gun, Night Market Song out in Silverlake, LA's hipster neighbourhood. There were a few places that we had meant to go to last time but couldn't make it to. One of those places was Petty Cash Taquería on Melrose. This time we had a specific reason to go as we had made contact with a guy called Bill Esparza. Bill is THE authority on all things Mexican, particularly tacos and mezcal, and his blog has a huge following. It turned out he was doing a mezcal tasting class at Petty Cash and we said we'd come down and join in, kill two birds with one stone. We arrived and sat down, ordering a few bits and pieces: fish tacos, chips and guac with uni or sea urchin. Bill then arrived with his cohort of mezcal heads ready for what was to be an important date in mezcal's history. We said our hellos and got stuck into the tasting session[1]. They'd managed to get hold of what's regarded in these circles as the best mezcal in the world, and something that had never been allowed into the States before, and they had got hold of all six variants, representing the different agave plants. Over the course of the next hour or so we tasted 10 or more mezcals and unlike any other tasting we've been to, there wasn't much spitting out going on. Once the tasting had finished Bill stayed around for a chat and it turned out that he was in Tijuana for the Baja food festival, a celebration of the culinary prowess of the area. He'd be there with a load of the chefs whose restaurants and trucks we'd been visiting on our trips. We hadn't planned on going to Tijuana but this was worth changing our plans for. We said our goodbyes, exchanged details and made arrangements to meet that Friday.

The final day of this first stint in LA came. We'd arranged to meet an old school breddo of ours, Al, who happened to be in town, so this had the potential to get messy. The breddos reunited; we headed to Melrose Avenue where lots of new cocktail joints had popped up and we embarked on something approaching a bar crawl. Whilst this was fun,

---

1 Mezcal is still a bit under appreciated in London but it was fascinating to learn about the techniques used to make it. Tequila for instance, is made from one particular type of agave plant and in one region within Mexico. Mezcal, on the other hand, is made from many varieties and all over Mexico though predominantly in Oaxaca and Chihuahua; this gives rise to a diversity and complexity that belies its popularity and really can be compared to whisky in its complexity.

it was not entirely sensible as we had a long drive down to Mexico the following day.

I woke up to my alarm screaming and a hotel room littered with bottles and cans. Clearly the party had come back to the hotel. The combination of a thumping head, having to get our shit together and now the added pain of having to clean the bomb site that was our hotel room, was not ideal. It transpired I'd passed out whilst Nud and Al carried on getting stuck in at the hotel (most out of character and a bit of a role reversal). Whilst I'd felt better, it was nothing a coffee and a bottle of water wouldn't sort out. Nud on the other hand was in all sorts of trouble. In the 15 years we'd known one another, I had never seen him so bad.

The sole reason for us having to get out of bed early was that we had a dinner reservation at a restaurant called Corazón de Tierra at 6.30p.m. that evening. The issue was that it was a four-hour drive to the border, another hour to cross, God knows how long to rent another car, a further two hours drive to Ensenada, check in, sort ourselves out and then drive the 45km (28 miles) into the Valle de Guadeloupe where Corazon de Tierra was situated. There wasn't a lot of margin for error, so this was not the most auspicious start...

We lugged our stuff into the car, dropped the roof down and headed out in the direction of Mexico via Highway 101. Immediately, Nud curled up in the foetal position in the passenger seat. I thought I would leave him be, but once he regained consciousness, I'd give him hell. (That's what friends are for, of course.)

The drive down to San Diego went almost without a hitch (only a couple of stops for Nud to throw up). We got to the border and parked up. Nud assured me that whilst he still felt terrible, he was through the worst of it. I was feeling very little sympathy at this point as I knew that I would now have to drive the whole way – driving in the States was one thing, but driving in Mexico was going to be a different kettle of fish altogether. It turned out to be a very smooth process; we passed immigration and were weaving our way through the barriers staring directly at the final bag check security and the guards' gleaming AK47s, when Nud suddenly started looking panicked and walking around in circles. Oh Christ, not now I thought. I could see his eyes moistening. He covered his mouth and started convulsing. He then projectile vomited in the middle of the hall, which was completely empty barring the guards with the aforementioned big shiny guns... and me. Thinking on my feet, I started shouting sorry to anyone who'd listen whilst trying to hastily wipe up the contents of Nud's stomach with a t-shirt I had pulled out from my bag. The guards quickly ushered us out of the hall, where we were greeted by sunlight pouring through an open door, above which read a sign: 'Welcome to Mexico'.

What an entrance...

Hello Mexico! We're back...

The road that took us down through Baja was absolutely staggering. We drove along the cliff, staring out across the Pacific. It was stupendously beautiful. (Unfortunately, Nud missed it all – as he had resumed the recovery position.)

Finally, after a very long day of driving, we got to Ensenada and found the hotel. Interesting would have been one word for it, though there are others far more appropriate. Our room, whilst clean, looked and felt like terrible things had happened in it and, given the proliferation of 'mujeres de las noches' touting their 'wares' outside our window, we didn't doubt this was the case. Amazingly, we had made the journey in great time and had an hour to sort ourselves out. Nud jumped into bed and pulled the covers over his head. I had started to feel something approaching sympathy by this point. Torturing him would be no fun at all in this state, he was a sitting duck.

When the time came to leave we headed back up the road, the way we had come, and turned into the Valle de Guadeloupe. This is the major wine area in Mexico and it had started to build quite a good reputation for itself; the terroir mirrored that of southern California. Vineyards stretched as far as the eye could see, in every direction. As magical as this vista was, there was a slight issue – all of the restaurants were located on vineyards which had no real addresses. If you didn't know where you were going, you were screwed. We found that the best way to locate anything was to find the town that it was near, El Porvenir in this case, and hope to drive around and find a sign. After a lot of driving down twisty vineyard lanes, we arrived with a minute to spare. The restaurant, Corazón de Tierra ('Heart of the Land'), was located at a vineyard called Vena Cava. We entered by a ramp through some nondescript buildings that had big oil lanterns guiding our way. It was then that we entered one of the most beautiful restaurants we had ever seen. Huge timbers jutted out of the ground, about 25 feet (7.6 metres) high, and in between them sat enormous panes of glass. The end of the building was completely open and looked out over the gardens which grew all of the restaurant's produce and the view extended down to the valley where the sun was setting over the Pacific. The kitchen at the other end was built out of rocks, with a huge fire pit at its centre. It was breathtaking. We don't know if it was the after effects of the previous night or the fact that we were knackered but it made us both really emotional.

The first thing we were offered was a glass of wine, all produced in-house, of course. Given his fragile state, Nud opted out of this and asked the bamboozled sommelier for a large glass of milk. Still, that meant that I could drink all the wine and Nud could drive home. Every cloud...

The meal was faultless. Incredible produce and cleverly put together by a brilliant team of chefs. This was what we'd travelled all this way for; modern interpretations of classic Mexican food, with exceptional local produce. A true highlight of the whole trip. A stunning experience all round and if you can go, you should.

Before we left Ensenada, we had a full day of eating planned. Ensenada is one of the most incredible places for seafood on earth. In fact, eight out of 10 of the world's most expensive seafood come from here – abalone, urchin and tuna. Until a couple of decades ago, these seafood were all exported to Japan, but then Mexican chefs, such as Benito Molina (Manzanilla) opened restaurants that celebrated the diversity of the local catch. In Ensenada, we were in the eye of the hurricane of our research trip.

Nud, Chris and Ms Sabina Bandera

First stop was Mariscos La Guerrerense, from Ms. Sabina Bandera, a world famous street stall, she was celebrated for her seafood tostadas and rightly so. Her guys turned up with bags of urchins, clams, oysters and sea snails, all pulled straight out of the sea and prepped ceviche-style before our eyes, alongside 30 of her salsas to choose from. It was utterly sensational – neither of us had tasted flavours like it before – sea urchins with pismo clams and chilli peanut oil, fresh and creamy oysters, it was a total revelation. The next stop was Tacos El Fenix, these guys were famous for their Baja fish tacos; freshly fried fish, shredded cabbage, pico and salsa. It's often said that it's the simplest things that bring you the most pleasure and this was a classic example.

The final stop before lunch was to El Pizón to visit Alan Pasiano, he sells uni tostadas at the far end of the town. What's more remarkable, however, was this guy's story. Until a few years ago, the majority of the food caught and landed in Ensenada would be transported to Japan. It was seen as the epicentre of the sea urchin universe and this guy was the uni (as it's called in Japan) king. He travelled to Japan and became the uni king there too. This guy was a rock star but he became addicted to drugs and disappeared for 20 years. He then came out of this torpor, moved back to Ensenada and restarted his original plan all over again. Unbelievable.

It was now just about time for lunch and we had a booking at Manzanilla, one of the most celebrated restaurants in the area. We opted for the 10-course tasting menu that included Smoked abalon and Bluefin tuna. We then managed to squeeze one more lunch in at Deckman's, an impossibly romantic open air restaurant under a tree in a vineyard that was wasted on us, before heading back up towards Tijuana.

We had arranged to meet Bill in the lobby of the Grand Hotel Tijuana where the conference was taking place. All the chefs were in town to do demos and cook a big banquet on Saturday to showcase the produce and culinary philosophy of this region. It was a who's who of chefs at the forefront of the cutting edge of Mexican food in California. There was Wes Avila from Guerrilla Tacos, Carlos Salgado from Taco María in Orange County, Ray Garcia from Broken Spanish and B.S. Taquería, Eddy Ruiz co-owner of Corazón y Miel, oh, and us. The plan was that Bill would take all of us to some spots he knew exemplified particular styles of tacos, which we would never have found ourselves in a million years.

The first place we went to served the best tacos al pastor that the city had to offer. The place was buzzing with locals, people coming and going the whole time. The second joint was a tiny little place with a simple wood grill and a tiny ramshackle extraction unit. There were about 15 of us and we joked that these guys would be completely in the weeds with the amount of orders they were about to receive. Not a bit of it. They went from doing nothing to slinging out tacos at a rate that was scarcely believable. These were some of the best carne asada tacos we had ever tasted. At this point the group decided that we all needed beer so we headed to a nighttime container yard. There was an incredible selection of craft beers, much of it brewed in situ. We sampled more than a few before the party started to break up. One of the plans was to stay up until 3a.m. as there was a stall that had its opening hours from 3–4.30a.m. on a Friday and Saturday. Unfortunately, we didn't manage to stay up that late so we're unable to report on what kind of alchemy this guy was up to, to enable this fantasy lifestyle.

The next morning, we headed back up the coast to LA completely inspired by our trip. We had seen what we needed to see and were bursting with ideas, not just for food but for everything we wanted to achieve. This had been a classic trip, Baja was majestic and California was as great as ever. Now it was time to do some real work and try to do justice to all we'd seen[2].

2 (We still get this nagging feeling that one day we will get found out. Surely, we can't enjoy what we do for a living this much. If it does all go to pop and breddos Tacos is no more, then at least this book will stand as some sort of testament to us that this did all actually happen.)

# BARBACOA BEEF CHEEKS

*This was one of breddos Tacos' first classic slow-cooker dishes. Cook it overnight and then use the spoon test to see whether the cheeks are done – basically, if you can cut through the cheeks with a teaspoon, then you're in business.*

1. Blend together the ancho chillies (including their soaking water), garlic, coffee, olive oil, cayenne, cumin, paprika, sugar, salt and pepper. Cover the beef cheeks with this paste and leave overnight or up to 24 hours, refrigerated.

2. An hour before you're ready to cook, take the cheeks out of the fridge to come up to room temperature. Preheat the oven to 140°C (275°F/Gas 1) or switch your slow cooker onto low.

3. In the meantime, heat the rapeseed oil in a frying pan and when very hot, sear the cheeks (leave the marinade in the bowl) in the hot oil until browned all over and caramelized, about 3 or 4 minutes. Put the cheeks into an ovenproof dish, with the marinade from the bowl, the stout and water, and put into the oven, covered, for 4 hours or until the cheeks are melt-apart tender. If you're using a slow cooker, put everything into the slow cooker dish and cook on low for 12 hours.

4. When the cheeks are done, take them out of the oven or slow cooker and let them rest for 30 minutes, then pull apart with two forks.

5. To serve, warm up you tortillas in a dry frying pan. Fill them with the meat, pico de gallo and sour cream, and garnish with coriander and limes.

## INGREDIENTS

**SERVES 6**

3 ancho chillies, soaked in hot water for 30 minutes
6 garlic cloves, chopped
1 tablespoon espresso coffee granules
4 tablespoons olive oil
4 tablespoons cayenne pepper
2 teaspoons ground cumin
1 teaspoon smoked sweet paprika
1 tablespoon sugar
1 tablespoon sea salt
1 tablespoon freshly ground black pepper
3kg (6lb 8oz) beef or ox cheek (ask your butcher to trim and clean it for you)
2 tablespoons rapeseed oil
1 x 440ml (16fl oz/scant 2 cups) can of stout or porter
200ml (7fl oz/scant 1 cup) water
18 corn tortillas (see page 16)
5 tablespoons pico de gallo (see page 132)
125ml (4fl oz/½ cup) sour cream
a handful of coriander (cilantro), chopped
2 limes, quartered

# PASTRAMI, SAUERKRAUT & RUSSIAN DRESSING

*This recipe takes the classic New York sandwich, The Reuben, and applies it to Mexican food. It's easy to prepare and a great lunch alternative.*

## INGREDIENTS

### SERVES 4

2 tablespoons butter
4 jalapeños, finely sliced
300g (10½oz) thick-cut pastrami
8 rye tortillas (see page 15), or corn tortillas
  (see page 16)
50g (1¾oz) Swiss cheese
4 tablespoons sauerkraut
4 tablespoons Russian dressing (see page 133)

1. Melt the butter in a frying pan and fry the jalapeños over a medium heat for 3 minutes. Add the pastrami and cook for 2 minutes, until slightly crispy, then set aside.

2. Working in batches of 2, warm up your tortillas in the frying pan. Add a quarter of the Swiss cheese to each batch so it begins to warm up and melt. Once the cheese has slightly melted, add some sauerkraut and some pastrami and jalapeño mixture.

3. Using a spatula, take each tortilla out of the pan and put on a serving dish. Spoon the Russian dressing over the top and repeat the process for the rest of the tortillas.

## SUNDAY SHORT-RIB BARBACOA NACHOS

*These are the ultimate Sunday comfort food, and are a great way of using up some short-rib (see page 20) or barbacoa (see page 31) that you have left over. The recipe below is a guide – feel free to raid your fridge and use up whatever you might have left. Quite often the best Sunday nachos I've had were created through total lack of direction.*

*This recipe is all about layering your ingredients. Unlike most other nachos, we like to design ours like a lasagne, using the chips as lasagne sheets, the meat and beans as the ragù and the cheese as the béchamel. The results are exactly what you want on a lazy Sunday night.*

1. Preheat the oven to 180°C (350°F/Gas 4). Line the bottom of a large ovenproof pan or dish with some of the meat mixture, then layer some chips over the top, then add some sour cream and Cheddar. Repeat the meat, chips, sour cream, cheese process until you get almost to the top of your pan or dish (make sure you have a little sour cream and cheese left over). Add the refried beans layer, then even more cheese.

2. Put into the oven for 20 minutes, then take out and add a layer of guacamole, followed by the pico de gallo then more sour cream.

3. Squeeze the lime juice over the top and garnish with coriander. Serve with a spoon.

## INGREDIENTS

**SERVES 2 AS A MAIN MEAL | 4 AS A SNACK**

200g (7oz) braised meat (short-rib, brisket, barbacoa etc.)
1 x 200g (7oz) bag of salted corn tortilla chips
100ml (3½fl oz/scant ½ cup) sour cream
250g (9oz) mature Cheddar cheese, grated
100g (3½oz/½ cup) refried beans (see page 140)
100g (3½oz/½ cup) guacamole (see page 133)
100ml (3½fl oz/scant ½ cup) pico de gallo (see page 132)
juice of 1 lime
coriander (cilantro), to garnish

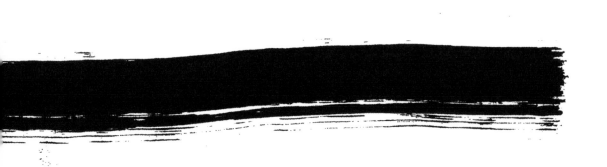

## RED CURRY PASTE BRAISED BEEF SHORT-RIB TACO WITH PINEAPPLE NAM PRIK RELISH BY JOHN CHANTARASAK

### INGREDIENTS

**For the pineapple 'nam prik' relish:**

2 long green chillies

2-3 green bird's-eye chillies

2-3 garlic cloves, peeled

sea salt

60g (2oz) pineapple, diced

1 tablespoon lime juice

1 tablespoon fish sauce

1 tablespoon caster (superfine) sugar

**For the red curry paste:**

a pinch of salt

7 long red dried Thai chillies, seeds removed,
   soaked in cold water for 15-20 minutes

1 tablespoon finely chopped galangal

2 tablespoons finely chopped lemongrass, outer
   layers removed

1 teaspoon finely chopped coriander (cilantro) root,
   cleaned and scraped

3 tablespoons diced Thai red shallot or banana shallot

3 tablespoons diced garlic

1 teaspoon shrimp paste

3 tablespoons vegetable oil

1 tablespoon palm sugar

2 tablespoons fish sauce

400ml (14fl oz/1¾ cups) coconut milk, fresh or tinned
with at least 70% coconut content

400ml (14fl oz/1¾ cups) chicken stock

500g (1lb 2oz) beef short-rib, sinew removed

8 rice flour tortillas

fresh kaffir lime leaves, very finely shredded

coriander (cilantro) stalks (to garnish)

1. Blacken the long green chillies over a gas flame using tongs. Set aside and allow to cool. Remove some of the blackened skin (not all as you want to have a smoky flavour) and the seeds from the chillies.

2. Pound the green chillies, green bird's-eye chillies and garlic with a pinch of sea salt in a pestle and mortar until smooth. Add the pineapple and the lime juice, fish sauce and caster sugar. Taste and adjust the seasoning. Set aside.

3. Make the red curry paste in a pestle and mortar by pounding the ingredients together until a smooth paste is achieved. Alternatively blitz the ingredients together in a food processor using a little water to achieve a smooth paste.

4. Preheat the oven to 160°C (300°F/Gas 2). Heat the vegetable oil in a heavy-based ovenproof pan over a medium to high heat. Add the curry paste and fry, stirring constantly, until the oil separates and rises to the surface. Add half of both the palm sugar and fish sauce and cook into the paste until incorporated, about 15-30 seconds. Taste a small amount of the paste again and adjust the seasoning: the paste should taste spicy, salty and slightly sweet. Add the coconut milk and chicken stock to the paste and bring to the boil, then immediately reduce to a gentle simmer.

5. Add the beef short-rib to the pan (it should be mostly, if not completely, covered in the liquid). Cover with a lid and transfer to the oven for 2 hours. The short-rib should be completely tender with the meat falling off the bone. Remove the short-rib from the pan and allow to rest.

6. Return the pan to the stove and reduce the red curry cooking liquor by a third. Reduce the heat to a low simmer. Taste the sauce and adjust the seasoning with the remaining palm sugar and fish sauce to suit the flavour combination you want to achieve. Then, using forks, shred the beef short-rib into fibres and return to the reduced red curry cooking liquor to keep warm.

7. Warm the rice flour tortillas in the oven for 2-3 minutes.

8. Serve by spooning the shredded beef into tortillas with a little red curry cooking liquor spooned over. Top with the pineapple 'nam prik' relish and garnish with finely shredded kaffir lime leaves (the finer the better) and coriander stalks.

# POULTRY

# &GAME

## YUCATAN-STYLE CHICKEN AND MANGO HABANERO SALSA

1. Mix the marinade ingredients together in the jug of your blender and then pulse until you have a smooth paste. Score the chicken thighs and rub the marinade into them. Place in a non-reactive container, cover and leave to marinate for at least 6 hours in a refrigerator.

2. Fire up your hob (cook top) and put your ovenproof pan or griddle on it with a slick of oil. Preheat your oven to 200°C (400°F/Gas 6).

3. Put the chicken thighs on the griddle, skin side down, and cook for 6–7 minutes, occasionally moving them to ensure they don't stick. Flip them over, cover the griddle or pan with tin foil and place in the oven for 20 minutes or until they're cooked through, then take the cover off the pan and put back into the oven for another 10 minutes. Take the chicken out and leave to rest. Meanwhile warm up your tortillas in a dry pan.

4. When the chicken has cooled a little, take two forks to it and shred it into a bowl. Squeeze the juice of a lime over them.

5. To assemble your tacos, take a tortilla and put in a big pinch of chicken, a teaspoon of mango, lime & habanero salsa, a pinch of coriander, a couple of pickled habaneros, a teaspoon of crema on top, and a squeeze of lime.

## INGREDIENTS

**SERVES 4**

**For the marinade:**
1 tablespoon cayenne pepper
1 tablespoon smoked paprika
1 teaspoon dried oregano
1 tablespoon sea salt
1 tablespoon freshly ground black pepper
4 tablespoons orange juice
2 tablespoons allspice
4 tablespoons pineapple juice
2 tablespoons lime juice
2 habanero chillies, stems removed
2 jalapeño chillies, stems removed
3 tablespoons rapeseed oil

**For the chicken:**
5 boneless chicken thighs, skin on
juice of 1 lime

**For the tacos:**
12 corn tortillas (see page 16)
4 tablespoons mango, lime & habanero salsa
  (see page 135)
4 tablespoons coriander (cilantro)
pickled habaneros (see page 132), to taste
4 tablespoons crema (see page 140) or sour cream
4 limes, quartered

## SPATCHCOCK CHICKEN WITH YOGHURT, CHERMOULA, AVOCADO & CHILE DE ÁRBOL

*This recipe lends itself extremely well to charcoal barbecue cooking – it looks great and isn't at all hard to cook. However, don't just save it for the summer – it's also a great alternative to your typical Sunday roast.*

1. Put all the ingredients for the marinade into a blender and whiz to a smooth paste. Cover the chicken with the marinade and leave in the fridge for 12 hours, or overnight.

2. When you're ready to cook, get your coals medium hot (you should be able to hold your hand 5cm (2 inches) from the grill without it feeling too hot, and the coals should be white and ashy) and place the chicken, skin side down, on the rack. Cook for 15–20 minutes, then flip. Cook for another 15–20 minutes, until the juices in the thighs run clear when pierced with the tip of a sharp knife. (For oven cooking, place the chicken in a baking tray and cook at 200°C (400°F/Gas 6) for 35–40 minutes, then turn up the heat to 240°C (475°F/Gas 9) and cook for another 10 minutes to crisp up the skin. Place the chicken on a board to rest.)

3. Meanwhile, grill the flatbreads, lemon, red onion quarters and thyme, if using, on the barbecue or in a frying pan and pile up next to the chicken. Place the rest of the serving ingredients in separate bowls alongside and serve up, family-style.

## INGREDIENTS

**SERVES 4 OR 6 (DEPENDING ON THE SIZE OF YOUR CHICKEN)**

1 whole chicken, spatchcocked (see page 139, or ask your butcher to do this for you)

**For the marinade:**
200ml (7fl oz/scant 1 cup) yoghurt
juice of 2 lemons
5 tablespoons chopped mint
5 tablespoons chopped coriander (cilantro)
2 teaspoons chilli powder
1 tablespoon finely chopped ginger
1 tablespoon finely chopped garlic
1 tablespoon ground cumin
1 tablespoon ground coriander
1 tablespoon sea salt
1 tablespoon freshly ground black pepper
1 tablespoon rapeseed oil

**To serve:**
4–6 Dong's flatbreads (see page 15)
1 lemon, quartered
2 red onions, quartered
small bunch of thyme (optional)
6 tablespoons chermoula
6 tablespoons salsa de árbol
  (see page 136)
6 tablespoons tomatillo salsa
  (see page 135)
6 tablespoons salsa roja (see page 136)
mint leaves
coriander (cilantro) sprigs
1 avocado, thinly sliced

## CRISPY CHICKEN SKIN TOSTADAS WITH AVOCADO & ANCHO CHILLI OIL

1. Heat a frying pan over a medium heat and add the rapeseed oil. Put the chicken skin in, fat side down, and sprinkle the salt evenly over. Turn the temperature down and cook slowly for 7 minutes, or until the fat has rendered down and you're left with crispy chicken skin. Turn the skin over and repeat the process. Once the skin is done, remove and leave to drain on kitchen paper for 1 minute.

2. Take the skin, which should be flat and crispy, and break each thigh piece in half. Place 2 pieces of skin on each plate and spoon over some avocado mojo. Drizzle over some ancho chilli oil and serve.

### INGREDIENTS

**SERVES 4 AS A SNACK**

1 tablespoon rapeseed oil
skin from 4 chicken thighs
1 teaspoon flaky sea salt
8 tablespoons avocado mojo (see page 133)
4 teaspoons ancho chilli oil (see page 134)

## TRIPLE-COOKED HABANERO CHICKEN WINGS

*You'll need an oil-safe temperature thermometer for this recipe; they're worth investing in, as they help ensure that your food is cooked to the correct temperature. If the habanero sauce is too hot, feel free to replace with avocado mojo (see page 133) or rancheras sauce (see page 137).*

1. Season the chicken wings with a pinch of sea salt.

2. Heat the rapeseed oil in a deep pan or pot to 120°C (245°F). Add the wings and fry for 5 minutes, then remove them from the oil and leave them to drain on kitchen paper. Place in the freezer for a minimum of 3 hours. Then take the wings out of the freezer and fry again at 120°C (245°F) for 4 minutes. Repeat the draining process and freeze again for 4 hours. (The wings can now be stored frozen until you're ready to use them.)

3. When you're ready to serve, reheat the oil to 190°C (375°F). Add the frozen chicken wings and fry for 4 minutes, then drain and season with cascabel chilli salt and pepper. Mix the Stilton and mayonnaise together to make the blue cheese dip.

4. Spoon the habanero salsa onto a tortilla and place the wings on top. Serve with the lime quarters, coriander and celery sticks.

## INGREDIENTS

### SERVES 4

1kg (2lb 4oz) chicken wings, split into two (ask your butcher to remove any hair and the tip)
sea salt
500ml (18fl oz/2 cups) rapeseed oil, for frying
cascabel chilli salt (see page 132), to taste
freshly ground black pepper
100g (3½oz) Stilton or other blue cheese
150g (5½oz/scant ¾ cup) mayonnaise
habanero or Scotch bonnet salsa (see page 136), to taste
8 corn tortillas (see page 16)
2 limes, quartered
a handful of coriander (cilantro), finely chopped
½ head of celery, peeled and cut into 5mm (¼ inch) fingers, kept in ice-cold water

## TRIPLE-STACKED CLUB TOSTADAS WITH CHICKEN & BACON

*This is a comfort food tostada that's great to make when you have a bunch of ingredients that need using up in your fridge.*

1. Preheat your oven to 200°C (400°F/Gas 6). Shred the chicken with your hands into 4–5cm (1½–2 inch) pieces. Heat a frying pan, add a slick of olive oil and cook the chicken for 4–5 minutes. Set the chicken aside, then add the bacon rashers (slices) to the pan and cook until crispy, 3–4 minutes on each side.

2. Assemble your clubs on an ovenproof tray, starting with a tostada, followed by a spoonful of mayonnaise smeared over the surface, then refried beans, then some lettuce, chicken, bacon and pico de gallo. Season with salt and pepper. Now on top of this, add another tostada and repeat the process, step by step. Cover the top of this tostada with breddos hot sauce.

3. Put a mound of cheese on top, to cover the sauce, and place in the oven for 5 minutes, or until melted. Serve on plates.

### INGREDIENTS

**SERVES 4**

4 x 50g (2oz) cooked chicken breasts
olive oil, for frying
8 rashers (slices) smoked bacon
8 tostadas (see page 14)
2 tablespoons mayonnaise
200g (7oz/1 cup) refried beans (see page 140)
1 head cos lettuce, shredded
pico de gallo (see page 132), to taste
breddos hot sauce (see page 132), to taste
sea salt and freshly ground black pepper
250g (9oz) mature Cheddar cheese, grated

## BUTTERMILK-FRIED CHICKEN, PICO DE GALLO & HABANERO AÏOLI

1. Mix together the buttermilk and salt, then add the chicken thighs and leave to soak for 24 hours in the refrigerator.

2. The next day, combine the flour, panko, paprika, cayenne, chipotle, if using, allspice, garlic powder, onion powder, mustard powder and baking powder in a large bowl. Take the chicken out of the buttermilk and plunge it into the flour mix, making sure you pack the flour on with your hands so it sticks – it's messy, but it's worth it for the crunch. Leave the chicken on a wire rack for 10 minutes.

3. In the meantime, heat the oil in a deep pan or pot until it reaches 180°C (355°F) or the point when a small amount of flour sizzles when added to the oil. Add a few chicken pieces at a time and cook for 4–5 minutes, or until a probe registers 75°C (165°F) in the thickest part of the chicken. Leave the chicken on a rack to cool and drain.

4. Warm up your tortillas in a dry frying pan, smear them with some habanero aïoli, then place the chicken on top with a spoonful of pico de gallo and some more aïoli.

## INGREDIENTS

**SERVES 4**

**For the chicken:**
250ml (9fl oz/1 cup) buttermilk
1 tablespoon sea salt
8 boneless chicken thighs, cut lengthways in half

**For the seasoned flour mix:**
200g (7oz/3 cups) flour
200g (7oz/3 cups) panko breadcrumbs or good
  quality breadcrumbs
1 tablespoon smoked paprika
1 tablespoon cayenne pepper
1 tablespoon chipotle powder (optional)
1 teaspoon allspice
1 teaspoon garlic powder
1 teaspoon onion powder
1 teaspoon Colman's mustard powder
1 teaspoon baking powder
500ml (18fl oz/2 cups) rapeseed oil

**For the tacos:**
16 corn tortillas (see page 16)
6 tablespoons habanero aïoli (see page 138)
6 tablespoons pico de gallo (see page 132)

fried chicken

# CHIPOTLE ROAST CHICKEN WITH ACHIOTE, AVOCADO MOJO & JALAPEÑO SLAW

*We discovered this dish after Chris and I had eaten a dangerous amount of stewed meat tacos while travelling through Mexico. Neither of us wanted to eat any more slow-braised meat. So, when a menu including roast chicken presented itself, we both desperately wanted it. However, the menu also had short-rib on it, and the rule of the trip was that when we saw short-rib, we had to eat it. For one of us, chicken had never tasted so good. For the other, it was one step closer to gout...*

## INGREDIENTS

### SERVES 4

1 head of garlic
1 lemon, halved
2 sprigs of thyme
1 x 2kg (4lb 8oz) free-range chicken, giblets removed
3½ tablespoons cubed jalapeño & achiote butter (see page 135)
1 onion, quartered
1 carrot, chopped into rounds
1 large potato, peeled and chopped into 3cm (1¼ inch) cubes
3 tablespoons rapeseed oil

### For the marinade:

2 tablespoons sea salt
2 tablespoons freshly ground black pepper
1 tablespoon dried oregano
1 tablespoon thyme leaves
1 tablespoon smoked paprika
1 tablespoon chilli powder
zest of 1 orange
4 chipotles in adobo
1 tablespoon achiote paste
grated zest and juice of 1 lemon
2 tablespoons rapeseed oil

### For the sauce:

1 tablespoon flour
1 tablespoon marinade (see above)
100ml (3½fl oz/scant ½ cup) white wine
100ml (3½fl oz/scant ½ cup) chicken stock
1 bay leaf
3 tablespoons unsalted butter
juice of 1 lemon

### To serve:

1 quantity of chipotle & jalapeño slaw (see page 110)
1 quantity of avocado mojo (see page 133)
8 corn tortillas (see page 16)

1. Preheat your oven to 220°C (425°F/Gas 7).

2. Put all the marinade ingredients into a blender and blitz for 2 minutes. You may have to scrape down the sides of the blender.

3. Put the garlic, lemon and thyme into the chicken cavity. Carefully separate the skin of both chicken breasts to create two hollow pockets. Put the jalapeño and achiote butter into both breast pockets, pushing it as far down as you can go without overstretching the skin. The butter will prevent the breasts from overcooking. Rub the marinade into the chicken, making sure all the chicken is coated. You should have some marinade left over – save this for later.

4. Put the onion, carrots and potatoes into a roasting tray and pour over the oil. Put the chicken on top of the vegetables and place in the oven for 25 minutes, or until the chicken skin is crispy. Reduce the oven temperature to 175°C (325°F/Gas 3) and roast for another 40 minutes, or until the juices from the leg run clear when it's poked with a skewer.

5. Remove the chicken from the tray of vegetables and leave to rest for 15 minutes in a warm place. Then put the tray with the vegetables over the hob (cooktop) on a low heat. Add the flour and a tablespoon of the marinade to form a paste, cook for a couple of minutes, then add the white wine, stock and bay leaf. Take the garlic and lemon out of the cavity of the chicken and put them into the tray. Use a wooden spoon to scrape any browned bits from the tray, then cook the sauce until it's reduced by half, about 10 minutes. Take off the heat and add the butter and lemon juice. Pass the vegetables and sauce through a fine mesh strainer into a jug, pressing down on the garlic and vegetables to extract every last bit of flavour.

6. Place the jalapeño slaw in a side bowl or on the side of a serving dish. Put the avocado mojo into a bowl. Place the chicken on the serving dish with the jug of sauce, and serve with warm tortillas.

## DUCK CARNITAS, GEM LETTUCE, PLUMS & PICKLES

*This is an awesome dish to serve up at dinner parties or get-togethers as a canapé. By using baby gem lettuce as the tortilla (the Koreans call it Ssam), it feels light and healthy, but it always delivers on flavour. The best thing about this recipe is that you can use any leftover duck for grilled cheese sandwiches, nachos and salads.*

1. Cover the duck with the salt and pepper and leave overnight, covered, in the fridge.

2. The next day, preheat the oven to 160°C (300°F/Gas 2). Put the legs fat (skin) side down into an ovenproof frying pan and cook on medium heat for about 15 minutes. You're looking to render the fat from the legs and release their juices. Turn the legs over and add the onion, chipotles, dried plums, garlic, peppercorns, anise and duck fat. Cover the pan with foil and put into the oven for 2–2½ hours.

3. Take the foil off the pan and increase the oven temperature to 200°C (400°F/Gas 6). Cook the duck for a further 15 minutes, then take out of the oven and set aside to rest.

4. Prepare the pickles by macerating the sliced red onion and habanero in the lime juice. Set aside in the fridge.

5. In the meantime, prepare the baby gems by snipping off the roots and separating the leaves of the lettuce with your hands – you'll find they have a natural boat shape, perfect for filling with food.

6. Shred the meat off the duck legs, making sure to mash the garlic and chipotle into the cooking sauce and incorporating it into the meat. Fill each lettuce cup with a generous helping of duck, followed by a plum from the cooking sauce, some prepared pink pickled onions, sesame seeds and a squirt of lime.

## INGREDIENTS

**SERVES 4**

4 duck legs
3 teaspoons sea salt
1 teaspoon black pepper
1 onion, quartered
2 dried chipotle chillies
8 dried plums (use apricots if you can't find plums)
1 head of garlic
1 tablespoon whole black peppercorns
2 whole star anise
200g (7oz/scant 1 cup) duck fat
1 red onion, thinly sliced
2 large habanero chillies, deseeded, veined and thinly sliced
100ml (3½fl oz/scant ½ cup) freshly
   squeezed, strained lime juice
4 baby gem lettuces
white sesame seeds, to garnish
2 limes, quartered, to serve

## JERK QUAIL, MANGO LIME & HABANERO SALSA

1. Crush the allspice and peppercorns and blitz to a paste with the rest of the marinade ingredients. Set aside a teaspoon of the paste for the jerk glaze, then rub the rest of the paste into the quails and marinate for 4 hours, or overnight in the refrigerator.

2. To make the jerk glaze, combine the honey and sugar in a pan and cook until it has the consistency of syrup. Add the garlic and the jerk marinade and remove from the heat.

3. When you're ready to cook, preheat your oven to 200°C (400°F/Gas 6). Heat a slick of olive oil in an ovenproof frying pan, add the quails and sear until browned on all sides, about 5 minutes. Brush the quails with some of the glaze and continue to cook for another 3 minutes, then place in the oven to finish for 5 minutes.

4. When you're ready to serve, arrange the quails on a serving board and loosely drizzle some more glaze on them, followed by 1 tablespoon of the mango salsa per bird. Serve with tortillas and burnt spring onions.

## INGREDIENTS

**SERVES 4**

olive oil
4 quails
4 tablespoons mango, lime & habanero salsa
  (see page 135)
8 corn tortillas (see page 16)
bunch of burnt spring onions (see page 138)

**For the jerk marinade:**
1 tablespoon allspice berries
1 tablespoon black peppercorns
½ teaspoon ground cinnamon
½ teaspoon freshly grated nutmeg
¼ bunch of thyme, leaves picked
5 spring onions (scallions), roughly chopped
3 garlic cloves, roughly chopped
2 Scotch bonnet chillies, roughly chopped
1 tablespoon dark brown sugar
2 tablespoons dark soy sauce
juice of 2 limes
sea salt

**For the jerk glaze:**
125ml (4fl oz/½ cup) honey
125ml (4fl oz/½ cup) sugar
3 garlic cloves, crushed
1 teaspoon jerk marinade (see above)

THis PEN smells of ALMONDS

I LOVE you really!

## GUINEA FOWL WITH AVOCADO

1. Preheat your oven to 180°C (350°F/Gas 4).

2. Rub the guinea fowl with some oil, then sprinkle with salt, pepper, cumin and the dried chillies. Place in a roasting tray and cook in the oven for 1 hour. When it's cooked (when the juices from the thigh run clear when pierced with a skewer), remove from the oven and let cool for 10 minutes.

3. Warm the tortillas in a dry frying pan and add a carved slice of guinea fowl per tortilla. Top with the avocado, a dusting of chipotle powder and a squeeze of lime juice.

### OPTIONAL: GUINEA FOWL WITH GUINEA FOWL TEA

1. Once the guinea fowl is not too hot to touch, pull all the meat off the carcass and set aside. Put the carcass into a stockpot and brown with some oil for 5 minutes. Add the carrot, onion and celery and cook for another 5 minutes. Add the stock, bay leaf, thyme and peppercorns and cook on a medium heat until reduced by half, for about 20 minutes. Add the red wine and carry on reducing until you have a velvety sauce. Strain the sauce through a fine mesh sieve into another pan and set aside.

2. When you're ready to serve, place the guinea fowl meat in a saucepan and add a tablespoon of the sauce. Heat for 3 minutes, then set aside.

3. Pour a small amount of the reduced sauce into a shot glass or egg cup and serve as a beverage to accompany the taco. Then follow step 3 (above).

## INGREDIENTS

**SERVES 4**

1 guinea fowl, giblets removed
rapeseed oil
sea salt and freshly ground black pepper
1 tablespoon ground cumin
1 dried habanero chilli, finely chopped
1 guajillo or ancho chilli, finely chopped

**For the guinea fowl with guinea fowl tea:**
1 carrot, finely diced
1 onion, finely diced
1 celery stalk, finely diced
200ml (7fl oz/scant 1 cup) chicken stock
1 bay leaf
1 sprig of thyme
1 tablespoon black peppercorns
120ml (4fl oz/½ cup) red wine

**To serve:**
8 corn tortillas (see page 16)
1 avocado, finely sliced
1 teaspoon chipotle powder
1 lime, quartered

## BRAISED HARE WITH QUICK YELLOW MOLE

1. To make the mole, toast the cinnamon, peppercorns and cumin seeds in a dry frying pan until fragrant, about 3–4 minutes. Remove the spices and set aside. Fry the garlic, tomatillos, onions and tomatoes for 5–7 minutes. Put the vegetables and toasted spices into a blender with the drained soaked chillies (reserve the soaking water) and pulse until you have a thick paste. You might need to scrape down the sides of the jug or add some of the soaking water to loosen the mixture.

2. Heat the lard in an ovenproof pot and, when hot, add the spice paste. Cook over a low heat until fragrant – around 20 minutes. Add the chicken stock and cook for a further 30 minutes, until reduced by a third.

3. Lightly dust the hare pieces with flour. Heat a slick of oil in a frying pan over a medium heat, add the hare and cook for a few minutes until lightly browned. Remove from the heat.

4. Preheat your oven to 130°C (250°F/Gas ½). Add the pieces of hare to the mole pot, cover with a lid, and place in the oven for 10 hours. Remove from the oven and leave to cool, until cold enough to touch, then remove the hare from the pot and pull the meat away from the bones, being careful to retain the chunkiness of the meat. Put the mole back over a medium heat and bubble until reduced by half.

5. Warm up your flatbreads in a dry frying pan. Warm up the hare in a pan with a few tablespoons of the reduced mole. Once hot, place on the flatbreads with another tablespoon of the hot mole.

## INGREDIENTS

### SERVES 4

1 hare, jointed
a handful of plain (all-purpose) flour
olive oil

### For the mole:
1 teaspoon cinnamon
1 tablespoon black peppercorns
1 teaspoon cumin seeds
10 garlic cloves, peeled
10 tomatillos, fresh
1 large white onion, diced
2 small tomatoes, roughly chopped
10 ancho chillies, dry-roasted and soaked in hot water for 30 minutes
10 árbol chillies, dry-roasted and soaked in hot water for 30 minutes
2 tablespoons lard
1 litre (1¾ pints/4 cups) chicken stock

### To serve:
4 Dong's flatbreads (see page 15)

## PHEASANT, AVOCADO HOT SAUCE & GRILLED ROMAINE

1. Put the butter and a slick of olive oil in a large heavy-based pot and heat. Salt the pheasants, then add to the pan and brown all over for about 3-4 minutes. Remove and set aside. Add the onion to the pot and cook for 5 minutes, before adding the garlic and thyme. Cook for another 3 minutes before returning the pheasants, breast side up, to the pan.

2. Add the chicken stock, chipotle, wine, olive oil, paprika, oregano and the 2 teaspoons salt and enough water to cover the birds. Bring to the boil, then reduce to a simmer, covered, for about 25 minutes. Set aside to cool, then remove the pheasants and pull the meat away from the bones.

3. Pour 500ml (18fl oz/2 cups) of the cooking liquid into another pot and slowly cook until the liquid has reduced by half, for about 10–15 minutes. Add the shredded pheasant and cook for another 5 minutes. Set aside.

4. Now for the lettuce: heat a griddle pan until hot, for about 5 minutes. Add the lettuce and cook cut side down for 3 minutes. Set aside. To make the vinaigrette, whisk together the lemon juice, salt, black pepper, olive oil, red wine vinegar and anchovies.

5. Pull the lettuce leaves apart to make individual 'cups' and pour over the vinaigrette. Add the pheasant and avocado hot sauce, and serve.

### INGREDIENTS

**SERVES 4**

2 tablespooons butter
100ml (3½fl oz/scant ½ cup) olive oil, plus extra for frying
2 teaspoons sea salt, plus extra for the pheasants
2 pheasants, giblets removed
1 onion, diced
5 garlic cloves, finely chopped
1 tablespoon thyme leaves
200ml (7fl oz/scant 1 cup) chicken stock
2 dried chipotle chillies
175ml (6fl oz/¾ cup) white wine
1 tablespoon smoked paprika
1 teaspoon dried oregano

**For the lettuce:**
4 heads romaine lettuce, cut in half lengthways
   and the cut sides rubbed with olive oil
50ml (2fl oz/¼ cup) lemon juice
1 teaspoon sea salt
1 teaspoon freshly ground black pepper
3 tablespoons olive oil
1 tablespoon red wine vinegar
4 anchovies in oil, finely chopped

**To serve:**
8 tablespoons avocado hot sauce (see page 133)

mmmmmm breddos
mmmmmmmmm TACOS

# PORK &

# & LAMB

## COCHINITA PORK PIBIL, X NI PEK & SOUR ORANGE

1. If you don't have time to brine the pork, rub the meat with sea salt and allow to sit for 30 minutes.

2. Place the orange juice, achiote paste, garlic, guajillo, cloves and onion in a blender and blitz to a paste. Rub the paste over the pork and leave to marinate overnight in the refrigerator.

3. Preheat the oven to 160°C (300°F/Gas 2). Wrap the pork in the banana leaf or baking (parchment) paper. Place in a deep casserole dish and cover with foil twice to ensure no steam escapes. Cover with a lid and cook for around 2½–3 hours, or until meltingly tender. Remove the banana leaf or parchment and shred the pork and then gently stir together with all of the cooking juices.

4. Toast the tortillas in a dry pan, then scoop a little of the pork pibil into the centre of each one and garnish with the x ni pek, and finally some chopped coriander and lime wedges.

## INGREDIENTS

### SERVES 4

1 kg (2lb 4oz) boneless neck end pork shoulder, brined
    overnight in 10% salt-water brine (see page 139),
    or see step 1
sea salt
500ml (18fl oz/2 cups) sour orange juice, or
    half normal orange juice and half grapefruit juice
200g (7oz/1 cup) achiote paste
10 garlic cloves
100g (3½oz/½ cup) guajillo chillies, deseeded, deveined,
    and soaked in warm water for 10 minutes
2 cloves, toasted and crushed in a pestle and mortar
1 small white onion, roughly chopped
1 large defrosted banana leaf (optional)
12 corn tortillas (see page 16)
6 tablespoons x ni pek (see page 133)
chopped coriander (cilantro), to garnish
1 lime, quartered

## PORK BELLY CROQUETTES

*These croquettes take time to make, but they freeze really well and people do go crazy for them.*

1. Salt the pork belly on each side with 3 tablespoons of salt and leave in the refrigerator for 5 hours.

2. When you're ready to cook, preheat your oven to 120°C (250°F/Gas ½). Put the belly into a deep roasting tray and cover with the duck fat or oil. Add the garlic, peppercorns and a sprinkling of salt. Place a piece of baking (parchment) paper on top of the pork belly, then cover with two layers of foil. Place in the oven for 4–5 hours, or until just tender. Leave to cool for 30 minutes to 1 hour. When the belly has cooled, remove the spices and cut it into 2cm (¾ inch) square pieces.

3. Beat the eggs in a bowl and set aside. Mix the flour with the paprika and cayenne and add a pinch of salt. Get your cooking set-up ready: you should have one bowl with the flour mix, next to the bowl of beaten eggs, and finally, next to the frying pot, the breadcrumbs.

4. Heat the 500ml rapeseed oil in a heavy-based deep pot to 180°C (355°F). Put batches of 5–8 cooked pork belly squares in the flour mix, then in the eggs, then in the breadcrumbs. Fry until golden brown, for about 4 minutes. When ready, remove and place on kitchen paper to take away any excess oil. Repeat with the next batch.

5. Serve with habanero aïoli.

## INGREDIENTS

### SERVES 8

1.5kg (3lb 4oz) pork belly, skin and bones removed
sea salt
2 litres (3½ pints/8 cups) duck fat or rapeseed oil
10 garlic cloves, peeled
2 tablespoons black peppercorns
500ml (18fl oz/2 cups) rapeseed oil, for frying
50ml (2fl oz/¼ cup) habanero aïoli (see page 138), to serve

### For the coating:

5 eggs
200g (7oz/1¼ cups) plain (all-purpose) flour
2 tablespoons smoked paprika
2 tablespoons cayenne pepper
500g (1lb 2oz/6 cups) panko or good quality
  breadcrumbs

## CHICHARRONES WITH CASCABEL CHILLI SALT & GUACAMOLE

*Everywhere you go in Mexico, you see food carts with huge lengths of crackling (pork rinds) hanging from the roof. Mexican crackling is different from what we're used to in the UK – the skin is dried out in a low oven (or in the sun) until it's firm. It is then fried, which has a puffing effect, not dissimilar to a prawn cracker or poppadom.*

1. Preheat your oven to 90°C (195°F/Gas ¼). Place the pork skin on a rack over a baking tray and cook in the oven for 3–4 hours, or until dry to touch. Break the skin into 9cm (3½ inch) shards.

2. Heat the oil in a deep, heavy-based pan to 190°C (375°F) and add a piece of the skin. It should puff up immediately. Repeat with the rest of the skin, sprinkling the pieces with the cascabel chilli salt as they come out of the oil.

3. Serve with guacamole.

## INGREDIENTS

1 large piece of pork skin (all fat and nipples removed; ask your butcher to do this)
500ml (18fl oz/2 cups) rapeseed oil, for frying

**To serve:**
cascabel chilli salt (see page 132)
200g (7oz/1 cup) guacamole (see page 133)

## PORK BELLY, BLACK PUDDING, TOMATILLO SALSA & CRACKLING

### INGREDIENTS

1. Mix the salt and spices together and spread them over the meat side of the belly. Refrigerate for 24 hours.

2. When you're ready to cook, preheat the oven to 240°C (475°F/Gas 9). Rinse the belly and pat dry. Heavily rub the skin with salt, then place the belly in an ovenproof dish or roasting tray into which it will fit snugly, skin side up. Pour in the chicken stock, being careful not to get the skin wet (it needs to be dry to form the crackling). Cook the belly for 20–30 minutes, or until the skin blisters and crackles. Turn the temperature down to 150°C (300°F/Gas 2) and cook the belly for 3½ hours, or until tender. Once done, remove the pork and set aside to cool. Once cool, cut the belly into strips 10cm (4 inch) long and 4cm (1½ inches) wide and set aside.

3. Heat a frying pan over medium heat and add the black pudding. Fry until soft, but still malleable, for about 1 minute. Remove and set aside.

4. In the same pan, warm up the tortillas – once they are puffing up, place on your serving dish or plates. On each tortilla place a couple of slices of black pudding, a slice of pork belly and a drizzle of tomatillo salsa and breddos hot sauce. Garnish with coriander, if using, and serve.

**SERVES 4**

100g (3½oz) flaky sea salt, plus extra
1 tablespoon smoked paprika
1 tablespoon fennel seeds
1 tablespoon coriander seeds
1 tablespoon ground cloves
400g (14oz) boneless pork belly, skin on and scored (ask your butcher to do this)
1.5 litres (2½ pints/6 cups) chicken stock
250g (9oz) black pudding (blood sausage), thinly sliced

**To serve:**
8 corn tortillas (see page 16)
50g (1¾oz/¼ cup) tomatillo salsa (see page 135)
1 tablespoon breddos hot sauce (see page 132)
a handful of coriander (cilantro) leaves (optional)

THE TACO TACO TACO CORE

# PORK RIBS WITH PICKLED WATERMELON

*I make these ribs when I cook up a belly and save the belly ribs for the staff meal. They're great for when you have a barbecue or big gathering planned.*

1. Preheat your oven to 150°C (300°F/Gas 2).

2. Place a roasting tray over a medium heat. Add the oil and, when hot, add the onion. Cook for 5 minutes, stirring occasionally, then add the carrot and celery. Add the pork belly ribs and the beer, allspice, garlic, agave, cayenne, brown sugar, salt and pepper. Bring to the boil, then cover tightly with foil and place in the oven for 4 hours.

3. In the meantime, pickle the watermelon. Place the vinegar, chillies, salt, pepper, agave and coriander seeds in a saucepan, bring to the boil then remove from the heat and immediately pour over the watermelon cubes. Set aside for at least 1 hour to pickle.

4. After 4 hours, the pork should be fork-tender – take the foil off the tray and turn the oven up to 200°C (400°F/Gas 6) for 10 minutes. Carefully remove the ribs and place on a serving tray, then put the roasting tray over a medium heat and boil to reduce the sauce by a third.

5. Pour the sauce over the ribs or into a bowl. Scatter the watermelon over the pork. Serve with warm tortillas.

## INGREDIENTS

**SERVES 4**

**For the pork:**
1 tablespoon rapeseed oil
1 onion, chopped
1 carrot, chopped
1 celery stalk, chopped
2kg (4lb 8oz) pork belly ribs
1 bottle of Corona or Dos Equis beer
1 teaspoon allspice
1 head of garlic, separated into cloves
2 tablespoons agave syrup or honey
2 teaspoons cayenne pepper
1 tablespoon brown sugar
1 tablespoon sea salt
1 tablespoon freshly ground black pepper
8 corn tortillas (see page 16)

**For the watermelon:**
½ watermelon, cut into 3cm (1¼ inch) cubes (rind removed and also cut into 3cm/1¼ inch chunks)
100ml (3½fl oz/scant ½ cup) cider vinegar
2 long red chillies, finely sliced
a pinch of sea salt and freshly ground black pepper
1 tablespoon agave syrup
1 teaspoon coriander seeds

## GREEN CHORIZO & DUCK EGG

*People normally think of chorizo as being red, but in Mexico they make the most incredible, vibrant, green chorizo that tastes so much fresher, herbier and lighter than the red version. This is a great dish to eat at any time of day, not least the morning after a night of overindulgence, should you have some to hand.*

1. Heat a large frying pan over a medium heat. Put in the chillies and garlic cloves and cook, turning from time to time. Both the chillies and garlic should be soft and blackened in spots. Remove from the heat and allow the garlic cloves to cool, then peel them.

2. Pick all the leaves off of the coriander and parsley. Place the leaves in a blender along with the cooked chillies, garlic and vinegar, and purée until smooth.

3. Place the pork in a large mixing bowl and pour the green purée over it. Place the salt, cloves, bay leaf, oregano, cumin, coriander and black pepper in a spice grinder and grind to a fine powder. Sprinkle the ground spices over the pork. Mix together with your hands and leave to marinate in the refrigerator for at least 12 hours.

4. When you're ready to cook, set a large frying pan over a medium heat and add the marinated pork mixture. Cook, stirring frequently, for about 10 minutes, and taste to check the seasoning – adjust the salt, pepper and spices to your taste.

5. Take the pork off the heat and set aside. Warm a generous slick of oil in a clean frying pan and, when hot, add the duck eggs. Keep basting the top side of the eggs with the oil, ensuring they are evenly cooked.

6. To serve, place 2 tostadas side by side on each plate and put a tablespoon of pork on each tostada, followed by the duck egg on top. Sprinkle over the queso fresco and some coriander leaves, add breddos hot sauce to your taste and serve with lemon wedges.

## INGREDIENTS

### SERVES 4

6 serrano or jalapeño chillies
6 garlic cloves, unpeeled
1 large bunch of coriander (cilantro), plus a handful of leaves, to serve
1 large bunch of flat-leaf parsley
60ml (2fl oz/¼ cup) Moscatel vinegar
2kg (4lb 8oz) coarsely ground pork shoulder (ask your butcher to do this for you)
2 tablespoons sea salt
2 cloves
1 dried bay leaf
1 teaspoon dried Mexican oregano
¼ teaspoon ground cumin
1 teaspoon ground coriander
½ teaspoon freshly ground black pepper
rapeseed oil
4 duck eggs or large regular eggs
8 tostadas (see page 14)
4 teaspoons crumbled queso fresco (see page 140) or feta cheese
breddos hot sauce, to taste (see page 132)
1 lemon, quartered

## PRESA IBÉRICA, ROASTED MARCONA ALMONDS & SALTED CHILLI PASTE

*Ibérico pigs roam free for a large part of their lives, feeding on acorns that have fallen from oak trees in dehesas (pastures). This diet, combined with the natural exercise they get from being free to move wherever they wish, creates a truly unique flavour profile. If you have never tried Ibérico ham, find your nearest Spanish retailer and buy some immediately. Its flavour is astonishing. The presa cut comes from the end of the loin of the pig, next to the neck. Unlike most pork dishes, you want to serve it medium rare – due to the nature of the pig and the life it leads, this is totally safe.*

1. Put a cast-iron frying pan on a medium heat. Rub the presa ibérica with a thin layer of oil and salt. When the pan is hot, add the presa and the garlic. Cook for 3–4 minutes, then flip. Cook for another 3 minutes, basting with any juices that have run out of the meat. If you have a temperature probe, you need to test the meat after about 5 minutes of cooking – when it reaches around 55°C (130°F), take it off the heat and let it rest for 3–4 minutes. If you don't have a probe, hold your thumb to your middle finger and feel the area underneath your thumb – if the presa feels this tender, it's medium rare.

2. Remove the pork to a board and add the butter and 4 tablespoons of the veal stock to the pan. Cook for a further 3 minutes.

3. To assemble the dish, place 2 tostadas on each plate, followed by the mustard greens and a teaspoon of the salted chilli paste. Slice the presa at an angle into 5mm (¼ inch) slices and place on top of the mustard greens. Sprinkle the toasted almonds over, with a drizzle of olive oil, a spoonful of the reduced veal stock from the pan and a scattering of coriander.

## INGREDIENTS

### SERVES 4

500g (1lb 2oz) presa ibérica
1 tablespoon rapeseed oil
sea salt
3 garlic cloves, crushed
1 teaspoon butter
100ml (3½fl oz/scant ½ cup) veal stock or beef stock

### To serve:
8 tostadas (see page 14)
a handful of mustard greens, blanched in boiling
    water for 2 minutes and cooled in ice-cold water
salted chilli paste (see page 132), to taste
100g (3½oz/¾ cup) Marcona almonds, roasted in a
    dry pan for 5 minutes and split in half
1 teaspoon extra-virgin olive oil
a handful of coriander (cilantro) sprigs, to serve

TACO
TACO
VISION

## MUTTON BARBACOA WITH PEA MOLE

*I cooked this for 130 hungry street food traders at a Street Feast trader dinner. The only thing more daunting than cooking for customers is cooking for your peers. Luckily, I think they liked it. I strongly suggest you use this as a show-stopper for a big gathering.*

*This recipe works fantastically in a smoker – if you have one – but it works just as well in the oven.*

1. Put all the ingredients for the marinade into a blender and blitz on high speed. You may need to scrape down the sides of the jug after a couple of minutes to ensure everything is evenly mixed. Rub the marinade all over the mutton shoulder and leave to marinate in the fridge for at least 24 hours.

2. Take your mutton out of the fridge at least 1 hour before you serve, and preheat your smoker or oven to 110°C (225°F/Gas ¼). Put the mutton into a tray, wrapped in banana leaves or baking (parchment) paper, cover it twice with foil, and put into the oven for 8 hours. Check the tenderness – it may need another couple of hours. When you're happy with it, take the mutton out and let it rest for at least 30 minutes. Then shred it with two forks.

3. In the meantime, warm up your tortillas, and get ready to feast. Spoon some pea mole on each taco, followed by the shredded mutton, sour cream, pico de gallo, habanero salsa, coriander, lime juice and as much pickled habanero as you like.

## INGREDIENTS

### SERVES 6

½ mutton shoulder, about 2kg (2lb 4oz)

**For the marinade:**
1 teaspoon cumin seeds
1 teaspoon Mexican oregano
1 tablespoon ancho powder
1 tablespoon cayenne pepper
1 teaspoon chile de árbol
a big handful of chipotle powder
20 garlic cloves, peeled
a big handful of sea salt
a big handful of freshly ground black pepper
100ml (3½fl oz/scant ½ cup) rapeseed oil

**To serve:**
18 corn tortillas (see page 16)
9 tablespoons pea mole (see page 137)
6 tablespoons sour cream
6 tablespoons pico de gallo (see page 132)
6 tablespoons habanero salsa (see page 136)
4 tablespoons chopped coriander (cilantro)
1 lime, quartered
pickled habaneros (see page 132), to taste

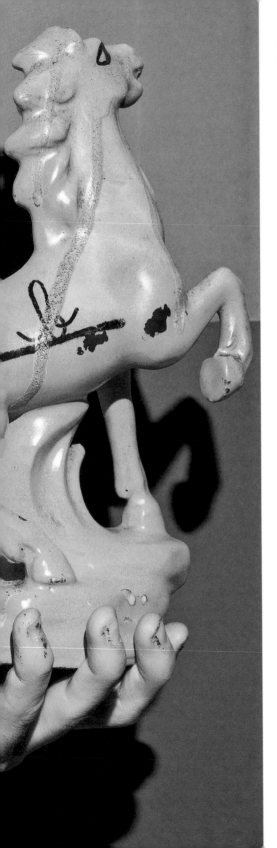

## CRUNCHY NUT FRIED SWEETBREADS & WILD GARLIC AÏOLI

1. To prepare the sweetbreads, soak them in milk overnight. Once you've done this, you'll need to remove the membrane surrounding them (it's a bit like skinning a sausage, a bit fiddly but a necessary process).

2. Make the aïoli following the method on page 138, substituting wild garlic for the garlic and adding it in at the end.

3. Heat the oil in a deep heavy-based pan to 190°C (375°F). Place the flour in a bowl, the buttermilk in a second bowl, and the panko breadcrumbs, almonds and sesame seeds in a third bowl. Dip your sweetbreads first in the flour, then in the buttermilk and finally, in the panko breadcrumbs. Drop them into the pan of oil in batches. Fry for around 4 minutes, or use a temperature probe, ensuring that the temperature has reached 70°C (155°F) in the centre of the sweetbread.

4. Serve with the aïoli on a tortilla.

## INGREDIENTS

**SERVES 4**

250g (9oz) lamb
  sweetbreads
550ml (1 pint/generous 2½
  cups) whole milk
500ml (18fl oz/2 cups)
  rapeseed oil, for frying
120g (4oz/1 cup) plain
  (all-purpose) flour
100ml (3½fl oz/scant ½
  cup) buttermilk
200g (7oz/2½ cups) panko
  breadcrumbs or good
  quality breadcrumbs
50g (1¾oz/½ cup)
  almonds, finely chopped
50g (1¾oz/½ cup) sesame
  seeds
8 corn tortillas (see page 16)

**For the aïoli:**

1 bunch of wild garlic,
  finely chopped
sea salt and freshly ground
  black pepper
2 large, free-range
  egg yolks
½ teaspoon English or
  Dijon mustard
1 teaspoon white wine
  vinegar
250ml (9fl oz/1 cup)
  sunflower oil or
  rapeseed oil

## BUTTERMILK-MARINATED LAMB WITH SPRING GREENS, SALSA VERDE & YOGHURT

1. Mix all the marinade ingredients together in a large dish and, once fully incorporated, add the lamb and thoroughly mix through. Cover and marinate for 24 hours in the refrigerator.

2. When you're ready to cook, drain the lamb from the marinade and preheat your oven to 160°C (300°F/Gas 2). Place your lamb in a roasting tray in the oven for 1½ hours, then turn the oven temperature up to 200°C (400°F/Gas 6) and cook for a further 20 minutes to crisp up the lamb. Remove from the oven and set aside to rest for 15 minutes.

3. Cook the spring greens in a pan of boiling water for 3 minutes. Remove and drain. Melt the butter in a frying pan over a medium heat, add the garlic and cook for 3 minutes, then add the spring greens, lemon juice and salt and pepper. Remove from the heat and set aside.

4. Warm up the flatbreads in a frying pan for 2 minutes on each side. Pull the lamb apart and place on the flatbreads. Move them to a serving platter and add the spring greens. Drizzle over the yoghurt and salsa verde and scatter over the pomegranate seeds.

## INGREDIENTS

### SERVES 4

1 leg of lamb, deboned and butterflied
500ml (18fl oz/2 cups) rapeseed oil, for frying

**For the marinade:**
1 litre (1¾ pints/4 cups) buttermilk
1 tablespoon sea salt
juice of 2 lemons
8 garlic cloves, crushed
1 tablespoon freshly ground black pepper
leaves from 2 sprigs of rosemary, finely chopped
2 tablespoons Dijon mustard

**For the spring greens:**
500g (1lb 2oz) spring greens, finely chopped
50g (1¾oz) butter
3 garlic cloves, finely sliced
juice of 1 lemon
1 teaspoon each of sea salt and freshly
   ground black pepper

**To serve:**
2 x Dong's flatbreads (see page 15)
100ml (3½fl oz/scant ½ cup) yoghurt
100ml (3½fl oz/scant ½ cup) shack salsa verda
   (see page 135)
seeds from 1 pomegranate

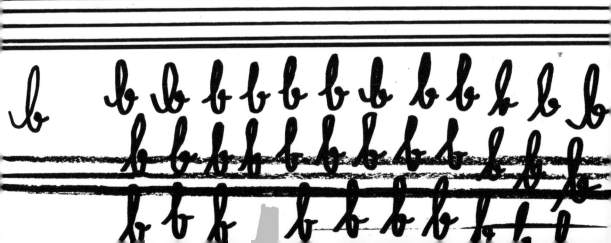

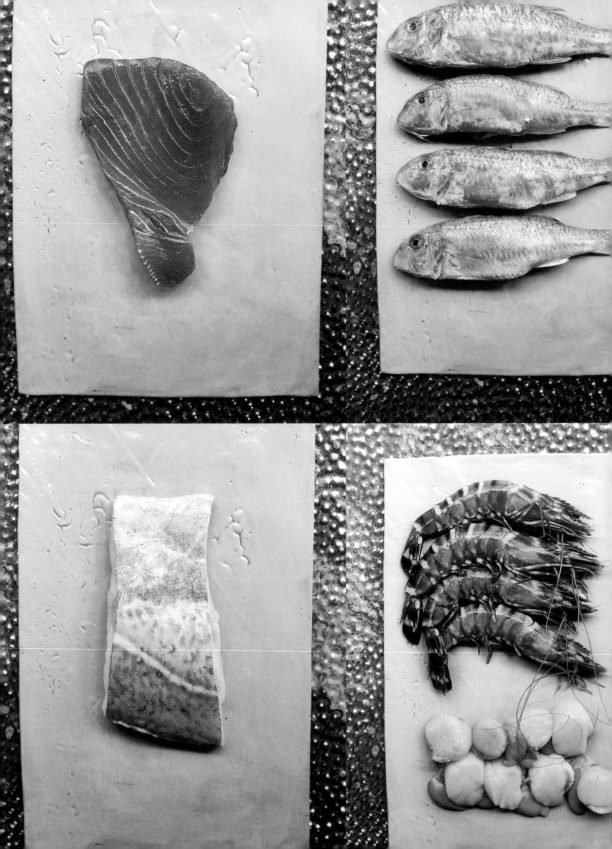

## OYSTERS WITH HABANERO MIGNONETTE

*We were asked if we wanted to serve oysters at the Milk and Honey Mercury Lounge, which was at Street Feast for a winter-long stint. I'd never used them before, but once I applied some Mexican flavours, this snack became a popular staple on the breddos Tacos menu.*

### INGREDIENTS

**SERVES 4 AS A SNACK**

8 native oysters
8 teaspoons habanero mignonette (see page 139)
1 lemon, halved

1. Shuck the oysters. Place the empty half shells flat side down on a serving tray and place the other half shell on top at an angle (see opposite).

2. Drizzle over 1 teaspoon of the mignonette per oyster and serve with half a lemon.

## TUNA TOSTADA, CHIPOTLE MAYONNAISE, BUTTER BRAISED JALAPEÑOS & AVOCADO

*This recipe takes inspiration from one of our favourite restaurants, Contramar, in Mexico City. It is the perfect lunch spot, serving uber-fresh seafood nestled away in the Roma district. Its tuna tostada is an unforgettable dish for those who have been there.*

1. To make the soy glaze, combine the soy sauce, sake, mirin and sugar in a pan and cook on a medium heat for 3 minutes. Mix the cornflour and water in a small bowl, add to the soy mix and stir until thickened. Remove from the heat.

2. To make the jalapeños, put the butter into a pan with the jalapeños and cook on a low heat for 5 minutes. Remove and set aside.

3. Put 2 tostadas on each serving plate. Place ½ teaspoon of chipotle mayonnaise and a slice of avocado on each tostada.

4. Put the tuna into a bowl and pour over the lime juice, mixing it through to ensure all the pieces are covered. Take 2 slices of tuna, dip into the soy glaze, then place on each tostada. Place a few jalapeños on each slice of tuna and sprinkle over some sesame seeds.

5. Give the tostadas a further squirt of lime juice and serve.

## INGREDIENTS

### SERVES 4

**For the tuna:**
500g (1lb 2oz) sashimi-grade tuna, sliced across the grain into roughly 60g (2¼oz) portions
juice of 4 limes

**For the soy glaze:**
100ml (3½fl oz/scant ½ cup) soy sauce
100ml (3½fl oz/scant ½ cup) sake
100ml (3½fl oz/scant ½ cup) mirin
100g (3½oz/½ cup) granulated sugar
2 teaspoons cornflour (cornstarch)
1 tablespoon water

**For the jalapeños:**
50g (1¾oz) unsalted butter
3 jalapeño chillies, sliced thinly into rings

**To serve:**
8 tostadas (see page 14)
4 teaspoons chipotle mayonnaise (see page 138)
1 avocado, sliced
1 tablespoon white sesame seeds
1 lime, quartered

## SALT-BAKED TROUT WITH LIME & WATERCRESS

*If you've never salt-baked a fish, I strongly encourage you to do so now. The salt intensifies the sweetness of the fish and acts as a casing in which the fish steams.*

1. Stuff the cavity of each trout with the thyme, rosemary and garlic and a lime each.

2. Preheat your oven to 200°C (400°F/Gas 6). You need two baking trays, big enough to hold a trout each. Line each baking tray with baking (parchment) paper. Place the salt in a bowl, add the water to dampen, then mix in the egg whites. You're looking for a clay-like texture. Divide the mixture in half. Place half of each mixture onto each baking tray and then place the trouts on top of the salt. Cover the trouts with the remaining salt, ensuring that they are completely covered. Sprinkle more water over the salt to dampen.

3. Bake the fish in the preheated oven for 40 minutes. To make sure they're cooked, prod a skewer through the crust and into the fish. It should come out hot to the touch. When the fish are cooked, take them out of the oven and crack open the crust. Carefully remove the fish whole and set aside, or remove the fish flesh to serve.

4. To assemble the dish, place a forkful of trout on each tostada, followed by some watercress, chilli flakes, tomatoes, yoghurt and lime wedges.

## INGREDIENTS

### SERVES 4

2 trout, gutted and cleaned
4 sprigs of thyme
2 sprigs of rosemary
4 garlic cloves, peeled
2 limes, finely sliced

### For the salt crust:

3kg (6lb 8oz/11 cups) fine sea salt
100ml (3½fl oz/scant ½ cup) water
4 egg whites

### To serve:

8 tostadas (see page 14)
100g (3½oz) watercress
chilli flakes
12 cherry tomatoes, halved
100ml (3½fl oz/scant ½ cup) Greek yoghurt
1 lime, quartered

## SCALLOP AGUACHILE

*You can use the marinade for this aguachile on most firm white fish, as long as it's extremely fresh.*

1. In a pestle and mortar, combine all the marinade ingredients.

2. Shuck the scallops and discard the orange coral. Wash the white muscle and slice it in half horizontally, and then again, so you double the number of scallop pieces. In a serving dish, mix the scallops with the marinade.

3. Sprinkle the onion and chilli flakes over the scallops. Place a couple of tostadas by each plate.

## INGREDIENTS

**SERVES 4 AS A SNACK**

4 fresh scallops
1 red onion, very finely sliced and soaked in ice-cold water for 10 minutes
2 teaspoons dried chilli flakes, to serve
8 tostadas (see page 14) or chicharrones (see page 65)

**For the marinade:**
juice of 1 lime
2 tablespoons orange juice
2 tablespoons grapefruit juice
1 teaspoon mezcal (optional)
1 teaspoon sea salt
2 tablespoons chopped coriander (cilantro)
2 tablespoons deseeded and finely diced cucumber

## GRILLED WHOLE RED MULLET
## WITH THAI DIPPING SAUCE

*The inspiration for this dish comes from the legendary Pong's restaurant barbecue on Thong Nai Pan Noi on Koh Samui, an idyllic paradise in Thailand that became my home for months on end, year after year, during my university days. At Pong's they served this dipping sauce with mussels at their weekly Wednesday barbecue. It's a revelation – the sweet, spicy, salty kick of flavours is so unexpected and my tastebuds have never been the same again. Here I have replaced the mussels with a British classic, red mullet.*

1. Make the Thai dipping sauce by combining all the ingredients in a bowl.

2. Preheat your grill and brush on some oil. Score the skin of each fish, then stuff the fish with the coriander stalks and lime slices. Rub some oil into the skin and sprinkle the salt and white pepper evenly over both sides.

3. Once the grill is hot, add the fish and cook for 4–5 minutes – when a fish slice will easily lift the fish off the grill, it's ready to be turned. Cook the other side of the fish for another 3–4 minutes – it's cooked when the flesh pulls away from the bone easily.

4. Warm up the flatbreads in a frying pan for 2 minutes on each side. Put 2 fish on each flatbread, with a couple of tablespoons of the dipping sauce, some coriander, mint and glutinous rice powder.

## INGREDIENTS

**SERVES 4**

**For the red mullet:**
rapeseed oil
4 whole red mullet, scaled, cleaned and gutted
4 tablespoons chopped coriander (cilantro) stalks
2 limes, sliced
2 teaspoons sea salt
2 teaspoons white pepper

**For the Thai dipping sauce:**
120ml (4fl oz/½ cup) freshly squeezed lime juice
120ml (4fl oz/½ cup) fish sauce
2 tablespoons palm sugar
2 tablespoons chopped coriander (cilantro)
2 tablespoons finely chopped Thai shallots
1 tablespoon ground dried bird's-eye chillies
2 teaspoons toasted and ground glutinous rice powder
  (see page 139)

**To serve:**
2 Dong's flatbreads (see page 15)
4 tablespoons chopped coriander (cilantro)
2 tablespoons chopped mint
2 teaspoons toasted and ground glutinous rice powder
  (see page 139)

# CRAB TOSTADA, ÁRBOL & TARRAGON

## INGREDIENTS

**SERVES 4**

1 x 454g (1lb) tub of freshly picked white
 crabmeat
1 small cucumber, deseeded and finely
 chopped
1 bunch of chervil, finely chopped
1 bunch of tarragon, finely chopped
grated zest of 1 lemon
2 tablespoons mayonnaise
1 teaspoon wholegrain mustard
1 tablespoon poppy seeds
a pinch of chilli flakes
2 teaspoons butter, melted
8 tostadas (see page 14)
breddos hot sauce (see page 132), to taste
2 limes, quartered
a few sprigs coriander (cilantro), to serve

1. Sift through the crab to ensure that there's
no shell in there. Put it into a bowl and
combine with the cucumber, chervil,
tarragon and lemon zest.

2. In another bowl stir together the
mayonnaise and mustard. Add the crabmeat
mixture, along with the poppy seeds and
chilli flakes, and combine.

3. Spoon some melted butter onto a tostada
and put the crabmeat on top. Serve with a
wedge of lime, some breddos hot sauce and
some coriander.

## LEMON SOLE CEVICHE WITH ÁRBOL, GRAPEFRUIT & RED ONION

### INGREDIENTS

#### SERVES 4

600g (1lb 5oz) lemon sole, skinned and trimmed
sea salt
100ml (3½fl oz/scant ½ cup) leche de tigre
   (tiger's milk) (see page 137)
1 large red onion, very finely sliced and soaked
   in ice-cold water for 5 minutes
a few coriander (cilantro) sprigs, leaves
   finely chopped
½ grapefruit, segmented, peeled and cut into
   1cm (½ inch) cubes
1 jalapeño chilli, deseeded and finely chopped
1 chile de árbol, finely sliced
4 tostadas (see page 14)
1 lime, quartered

1. Cut the fish into uniform strips of around 4 x 3cm
(1½ x 1¼ inches). Place in a large bowl, add a good pinch
of salt and mix together gently with a metal spoon. Leave
this for a minute, then pour over the tiger's milk and
combine gently with the spoon. Leave the fish to 'cook'
in this marinade for another minute.

2. Add the drained onions, coriander, grapefruit, jalapeño
and árbol chillies to the fish. Mix together gently
with the spoon.

3. Place a tostada on each plate and spoon in some
lemon sole ceviche. Serve with lime.

## JALAPEÑO & MINT CRUSTED FISH

### INGREDIENTS

#### SERVES 4

1 stick of cinnamon
10 black peppercorns
4 cloves
90g (3¼oz) coriander (cilantro) leaves
20g (½oz) mint leaves
5cm (2 inch) piece of fresh ginger
2 large garlic cloves
2 jalapeño chillies
4 teaspoons lime juice
2 tablespoons olive oil
1 teaspoon salt
2 tablespoons double (heavy) cream
4 thick fillets of cod or pollack, skin on
olive oil, for frying

**To serve:**
4 tablespoons chipotle & jalapeño slaw (see page 110)
2 limes, quartered
4 tostadas (see page 14)

1. Grind the cinnamon, peppercorns and cloves in a
pestle and mortar. Place the herbs in a food processor
with the ginger, garlic, jalapeños, lime juice, oil, ground
spices and salt. Whiz until smooth, then stir in the cream.
Taste and adjust the seasoning. Pour the mixture over the
fish and leave to marinate for 1 hour in the refrigerator.

2. When you're ready to cook, heat some olive oil in
a frying pan over medium heat. Add the fish, skin side
down, and cook for 3–4 minutes. The flesh will turn from
a translucent colour to white as it cooks. Once the fish
has turned white 60% of the way up, flip the fish and cook
for another 2 minutes. Then take it off the heat.

3. On each serving plate, place a handful of slaw in the
middle, followed by a fillet of fish, skin side up. Serve
with lime quarters and a tostada.

## SASHIMI SEA BASS, FISH SKIN CHICHARRONES, RASPBERRY VINEGAR, CHILLI & OLIVE OIL

*Making the fish skin chicharrones for this recipe really is worth it, but if you haven't got the time, this is still a great dish without them.*

### INGREDIENTS

**SERVES 4 AS A SNACK**

**For the sea bass:**
2 fillets of sea bass, skinned (reserve skin),
   pin-boned and cut into 4 x 3cm (1½ x 1¼ inch) strips
1 teaspoon extra-virgin olive oil
1 teaspoon sea salt
1 bird's-eye chilli, deseeded and very finely chopped
1 tablespoon raspberry vinegar

**For the chicharrones:**
skin from the sea bass fillets, all flesh and fat removed
200ml (7fl oz/scant 1 cup) rapeseed oil
1 teaspoon sea salt

**To serve:**
4 tostadas (see page 14)
1 lime, quartered

1. To make the chicharrones, preheat your oven to 80°C (175°F/Gas ¼). Place the fish skins on a lightly greased baking sheet and cook for 1 hour, then turn and cook for another hour. Once the skins are nice and dry, heat the oil in a frying pan to 190°C (375°F) and, when hot, add the skins – they'll puff up and soufflé within 45 seconds. Take them off the heat and season with salt immediately. Set aside. (Do not eat them yet!)

2. Put the sea bass into a bowl with the olive oil and salt. Mix through and add the bird's-eye chilli. Dip your index finger into the raspberry vinegar and apply a light coating to each segment of the sea bass.

3. Place 2–3 segments of sea bass on each tostada. Serve with the lime and a shard of the crispy skin.

## 'NDUJA STUFFED SARDINES, FENNEL, CONFIT TOMATO & RED CHILLI

### INGREDIENTS

**SERVES 4**

8 whole sardines, gutted
50g (1¾oz) 'nduja
1–2 tablespoons roasted garlic oil (see page 134)
sea salt
2 tablespoons extra-virgin olive oil
1 bulb of fennel, finely chopped
2 long red chillies, finely chopped
juice of 1 lime
200g (7oz/1 cup) confit tomatoes (see page 140)

1. Stuff the cavity of the sardines with the 'nduja, then brush the outside of the fish with the garlic oil and sprinkle salt all over.

2. Heat half the olive oil in a frying pan and fry the fish in batches. Cook for 3 minutes, then flip and cook for another 2 minutes or so. The fish is cooked when the bone easily pulls away from the flesh.

3. Dress the fennel with the remaining extra-virgin olive oil, salt, chillies and lime juice. Place 2 sardines on each plate, with a small handful of the fennel mixture and a spoonful of the confit tomatoes.

# BAJA FISH TACO

*Chris and I travelled up and down the coast of Baja California, in 2015, eating the best fish tacos known to man at crowded food carts dotted on street corners. The tacos were so cheap, one or two dollars, the fish fresh from the sea, coated in a crunchy light batter, garnished with shredded cabbage, and a choice of zingy, spicy and refreshing salsas. The taqueros here didn't use digital thermometers, nor did they have deep-fat fryers. Years of cooking fish tacos had given them an instinctive knack of cooking the fish perfectly every time.*

*This is our take on the Baja fish taco, and whilst it's not a like-for-like copy (as that would be impossible) it uses the best of British produce to recreate a Baja classic.*

1. Heat the rapeseed oil in a deep heavy-based pan to 190°C (375°F).

2. Make the batter by mixing together the flours, egg, baking powder, salt, chilli powder and oregano. Slowly pour in the sparkling water or beer and whisk until you have a batter-like consistency; ignore any lumps.

3. Dip one piece of fish at a time into the rice flour. Using tongs, dip the fish into the batter and then gently place the fish in the hot oil. Be sure to put the fish into the oil away from your body in case of oil splashes. Repeat with 3 of the other pieces of fish and cook for 4 minutes.

4. Take the first 4 pieces out of the oil and leave to drain on kitchen paper. Repeat with the other 4 pieces of fish.

5. Assemble your tacos by warming the tortillas, place a dollop of aïoli on them, followed by the fish, cabbage, pico de gallo, a couple of slices of jalapeño and some coriander. Sprinkle with cascabel chilli salt and add a squeeze of lime juice.

## INGREDIENTS

### SERVES 4

**For the batter:**
200g (7oz/1⅓ cups) rice flour
100g (3½oz/¾ cup) plain (all-purpose) flour
1 egg, beaten
1 teaspoon baking powder
1 teaspoon fine salt
1 teaspoon chilli powder
½ teaspoon dried oregano
200ml (7fl oz/scant 1 cup) cold sparkling water
 or light beer

**For the fish:**
500ml (18fl oz/2 cups) rapeseed oil, for frying
1 large pollack fillet, skinned and pin boned,
 cut into 8 evenly sized rectangular pieces
100g (3½oz/¾ cups) rice flour

**To serve:**
8 corn tortillas (see page 16)
100g (3½oz/scant ½ cup) lime aïoli (see page 138)
½ head white cabbage, finely chopped
100ml (3½oz/scant ½ cup) pico de gallo (see page 132)
1 jalapeño chilli, finely sliced
a handful of coriander (cilantro), leaves picked
4 limes, halved
cascabel chilli salt (see page 132)

## OCTOPUS 'AL PASTOR' & ROASTED PINEAPPLE

*This recipe calls for dipping the octopus in boiling water three times before actually adding it to the pot. This is something cooks in Galicia do to gradually introduce heat to the octopus – it prevents it from becoming rubbery.*

1. Make the marinade by blending all the ingredients together. You may need to scrape down the sides of the jug to ensure everything gets incorporated. Set aside.

2. To cook the octopus, fill a large stockpot with water and add the salt, garlic and onion. Bring to the boil. Using tongs, grab the head of the octopus and dip the creature into the water for a few seconds. Repeat this twice more, for both octopuses, then leave them to cook in the boiling water for 40 minutes.

3. Once the octopus is cooked, remove it from the heat and transfer it to a bowl of ice-cold water to prevent it cooking any further. Once cool, drain the octopuses and remove the tentacles. Place in a large bowl with the marinade and leave to marinate for 2–3 hours.

4. Get a grill or, better still, a barbecue hot and add the octopus tentacles. You're looking to create a quick char. While they are cooking, baste the tentacles with any leftover marinade.

5. Mix the pineapple, lime juce and habanero together in a bowl. Place the octopus on a serving platter and pour some mango habanero salsa over, with a few squeezes of fresh lime juice, coriander leaves and radishes served alongside.

## INGREDIENTS

**SERVES 4**

**For the octopus:**
6 tablespoons sea salt
3 garlic cloves
1 onion, quartered
2 frozen octopuses, defrosted

**For the marinade:**
2 garlic cloves
1 teaspoon sea salt
2 tablespoons achiote paste
1 onion, roughly chopped
1 tablespoon cider vinegar
1 teaspoon cumin seeds
3 allspice berries

½ pineapple, sliced into sticks, roasted
  in a dry frying pan or chargrill pan until blackened
juice of 1 lime
½ habanero chilli, diced
4 tablespoons mango, lime & habanero salsa
  (see page 135)
1 lime, quartered
handful of coriander (cilantro) leaves
4 radishes with stalks, halved

## XL TIGER PRAWNS & GREEN CHILLI SALSA

*These prawns are inspired by the ones that I used to eat
as a kid, made by my Mauritian auntie. We used to look
forward all summer to the day she'd cook these, and when
she did, we'd fight over them. I remember sucking every
last bit of buttery, spicy flavour out of the shells and heads
and pining for more. I've adapted the recipe a little, but
the Mauritian foundations are still there.*

1. Butterfly the prawns by slicing each one through the
spine and splitting it in two. You should see a black tube
like a vein running down the prawn – remove this.

2. Place the butter, garlic, jalapeños, red chillies, salt,
pepper and chilli powder in a saucepan and cook, stirring,
over a low heat until the butter has melted and everything
has combined.

3. Preheat an overhead grill to a high heat. Place the
prawns in a baking dish, flesh side up, and pour over the
butter mixture. Grill for 3 minutes, then flip the prawns
and cook for another 2 minutes. Remove the prawns from
the baking dish and set aside.

4. Pour the liquid out of the baking dish back into the
pan you melted the butter in, and cook for 5 minutes.
Pour this mixture over the prawns, sprinkle over the
coriander and squeeze the lemon quarters all over.
Serve with buttered sourdough.

## INGREDIENTS

### SERVES 4

8 extra large tiger prawns
100g (3½oz) butter
5 garlic cloves, finely chopped
2 jalapeño chillies, finely chopped
2 red chillies, finely chopped
a pinch each of sea salt and freshly ground black pepper
1 teaspoon chilli powder
2 tablespoons chopped coriander (cilantro)
1 lemon, quartered
2 slices of sourdough toast, heavily buttered

BLES

& SIDES

# HUEVOS RANCHEROS

## INGREDIENTS

**SERVES 4**

200ml (7fl oz/scant 1 cup) rancheros sauce
  (see page 137)
1 tablespoon rapeseed oil
4 free-range eggs
sea salt and freshly ground black pepper
100g (3½oz) Cheddar cheese, grated
4 Dong's flatbreads (see page 15) or 16 corn tortillas
  (see page 16)
100g (3½oz) guacamole (see page 133)
4 teaspoons sour cream
2 tablespoons roughly torn coriander (cilantro)
breddos hot sauce (see page 132) or salted chilli
  paste (see page 132), to taste
1 lime, cut into wedges
2 red chillies, finely sliced
4 tablespoons pico de gallo (see page 132)

1. Put the rancheros sauce in a pan and heat through
over a medium heat until piping hot, about 5 minutes,
then set aside.

2. Heat a frying pan on a medium heat. Add the oil
and let it heat up for 3 minutes. Crack the eggs into
the frying pan and cook sunny side up, basting the top
of the egg with the oil using a spoon, until the whites are
set but the yolks are still runny. Add some salt and
pepper to the eggs. Pour the rancheros sauce into the
frying pan with the eggs and sprinkle over the cheese.
Remove from the heat.

3. Warm up the flatbreads or tortillas and place on
4 plates. Spoon the guacamole and sour cream on top
of the eggs and then sprinkle the coriander over
everything. Serve with breddos hot sauce, lime wedges
and a scattering of chillies, with the pico de gallo alongside. Then dig in!

# CROQUETAS

## INGREDIENTS

**MAKES ABOUT 30**

2 tablespoons olive oil
60g (2oz) unsalted butter
½ small leek, finely diced
100g (3½oz) cured ham or salami, diced
60g (2¼oz/1½ cups) plain (all-purpose) flour
500ml (18fl oz/2 cups) whole milk, hot
nutmeg, to grate
freshly ground black pepper
2 free-range eggs, beaten
150g (5½oz/1½ cups) panko breadcrumbs or good
   quality breadcrumbs
25g (1oz) Manchego or other hard cheese, finely grated
1 litre (1¾ pints/4 cups) rapeseed oil, for frying

1. Heat the olive oil and butter in a heavy-based saucepan over a medium heat, add the leek and fry gently for a minute. Add 70g (2½oz) of the ham and cook until the leek has softened and the ham fat has begun to melt.

2. Turn the heat down, gradually stir in the flour and cook gently, stirring regularly, until it loses its raw flavour – this should take about 8–10 minutes. Gradually stir in the hot milk, beating it in well, until you have a smooth paste. Cook for another 15 minutes, until it has the consistency of smooth mashed potato, then fold through the rest of the ham and season to taste with a grating of nutmeg and some black pepper (you shouldn't need any salt). Transfer to a bowl and allow to cool, then cover, pressing clingfilm (plastic wrap) onto the surface of the sauce to prevent a skin from forming, and refrigerate for at least 2 hours.

3. Put the beaten eggs into a bowl, and the breadcrumbs with the cheese into another. With floured hands, roll spoonfuls of the mixture into cylinders and dip these into the egg, then roll in the breadcrumbs until well coated.

4. Heat the rapeseed oil in a deep pan to 180°C (355°F). Line a plate with kitchen paper. Fry the croquetas in batches for a couple of minutes until golden all over, then lift out with a slotted spoon and serve at once.

## GRILLED ROMAINE, PRESERVED LEMON, SOUR CREAM, PARMESAN, ANCHOVY & CHICKEN SKIN SALAD

### INGREDIENTS

**SERVES 4 AS A SIDE SALAD | 2 AS A MAIN COURSE**

2 large heads of romaine lettuce, cut in half lengthways
2 tablespoons melted butter
1 teaspoon sea salt
1 teaspoon crushed black pepper
1 teaspoon crushed dried chilli, such as árbol
juice of 1 lime
1 preserved lemon, roughly chopped
100ml (3½fl oz/scant ½ cup) sour cream
8 anchovies
100g (3½oz) Parmesan cheese shavings
drizzle of extra-virgin olive oil
4 tablespoons crumbled chicken skin (see page 44)
salted chilli paste (see page 132), to taste

1. Heat a griddle pan and brush the cut side of the romaine with the melted butter. Place the romaine cut side down on the griddle and char for 3 minutes – it should blacken a little. Take off the heat and put into a large bowl, with the salt, pepper, chilli, lime juice, preserved lemon and sour cream.

2. Place 2 romaine halves on each plate. Scatter over the anchovies, Parmesan shavings, a drizzle of olive oil and the chicken skin.

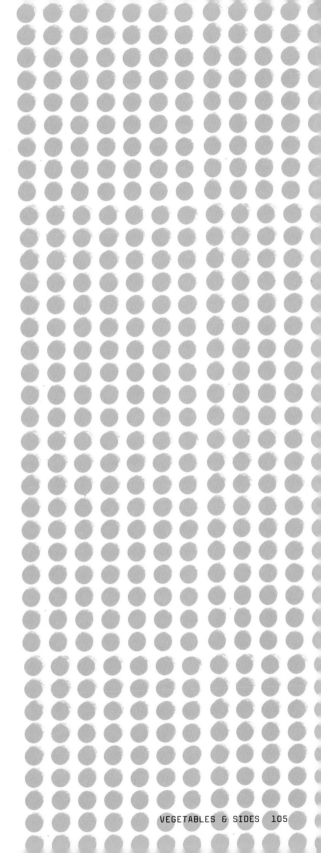

## TEMPURA VEGETABLES, LIME AÏOLI & EPAZOTE

### INGREDIENTS

**SERVES 4**

**For the batter:**
100g (3½oz/¾ cup) rice flour
1 egg, beaten
160ml (5fl oz/⅔ cup) cold sparkling water or light beer
1 tablespoon sesame seeds or poppy seeds
1 teaspoon chilli flakes, plus extra to serve
½ teaspoon epazote (see page 13), plus extra to serve

200ml (7fl oz/scant 1 cup) rapeseed oil
4 baby beetroot (beet), peeled and cut into
   5mm (¼ inch) wedges
4 baby carrots, peeled and halved
4 baby leeks, washed
8 kale leaves, cut into roughly 8cm (3¼ inch) squares
a handful of fennel tops
4 slices of pumpkin, roughly 5mm (¼ inch) thick and 8cm
   (3¼ inches) long
4 white mushrooms
salt and freshly ground black pepper

**To serve:**
8 corn tortillas (see page 16)
4 tablespoons lime aïoli (see page 138)
1 tablespoon coriander oil (see page 134)

1. In a bowl, whisk together the rice flour and egg, then pour in the water or beer. Try to keep it smooth. Add the sesame seeds or poppy seeds, chilli flakes and epazote.

2. Heat the rapeseed oil to 180°C (355°F). Dip the vegetables into the tempura batter using tongs, then lower them carefully into the hot oil in batches. Cook for 3–4 minutes, until golden, and remove with a slotted spoon to a tray lined with kitchen paper. Season with sea salt and some black pepper. Repeat until you have fried all of the vegetables.

3. Warm up your tortillas and place vegetables on each, followed by a big spoonful of lime aïoli, a sprinkling of chilli flakes, a little epazote and coriander oil.

## BAKED BUTTERNUT SQUASH WITH MACADAMIA, CHILLI OIL & QUESO FRESCO

### INGREDIENTS

**SERVES 4**

2 small butternut squash, each split in half, seeds removed
   and scored across the flesh
2 tablespoons rapeseed oil
sea salt and freshly ground black pepper
4 garlic cloves, finely chopped
1 teaspoon cayenne pepper
1 teaspoon chipotle powder
1 teaspoon dried oregano
4 sprigs of thyme
4 tablespoons of butter
100g (3½oz) queso fresco (see page 140) or feta cheese
100g (3½oz) macadamia nuts, halved, plus extra to serve
8 tostadas (see page 14)
1 tablespoon ancho chilli oil (see page 134)
50g (1¾oz) Parmesan shavings
4 tablespoons natural yoghurt
chilli flakes, to serve
small bunch of coriander (cilantro), to serve
1 lime, halved

1. Preheat your oven to 190°C (375°F/Gas 5). Place the squash halves on a large baking tray and drizzle the rapeseed oil all over. Generously season with salt and pepper, then sprinkle the garlic, cayenne, chipotle and oregano all over, including in the cavity of the squash, and place a sprig of thyme on each half. Put a knob of butter into each cavity, with another sprinkle of salt.

2. Put the tray into the oven and bake for around 20 minutes. Remove from the oven and flip the squash face down, then cook for another 20 minutes, until the pieces have blackened on top and the flesh is tender.

3. When you're ready to serve, scatter the squash halves with the queso fresco and macadamias and add a couple of tostadas on the side. Drizzle over the chilli oil, shavings of Parmesan and add a dollop of natural yoghurt and a few chilli flakes. Scatter over some coriander and add a squeeze of lime before serving.

# CHIPOTLE & JALAPEÑO SLAW

## INGREDIENTS

**SERVES 4**

**For the slaw:**
½ head of white cabbage, finely sliced
½ head of red cabbage, finely sliced
sea salt
1 small bulb of fennel, finely sliced
1 carrot, grated
125g (4½oz/½ cup) chipotle mayonnaise (see page 138)
a handful of coriander (cilantro) leaves

**For the dressing:**
50g (1¾oz) jalapeño chillies
25g (1oz) ginger, peeled and grated
25g (1oz) garlic cloves
25g (1oz) brown sugar
juice of 2 limes
25ml (1fl oz) soy sauce

1. Place the sliced cabbages in a colander and salt lightly – leave for 1 hour to draw out the moisture.

2. Meanwhile, to make the dressing, blitz all the ingredients apart from the soy sauce in a blender. Add the soy sauce gradually to the dressing until mixed in.

3. Transfer the cabbage to a serving bowl and add the fennel and carrot. Add the mayonnaise, coriander leaves and 50ml (2fl oz/¼ cup) of the dressing, and toss. Season with salt to taste, adding more dressing if needed.

# BABY GEM, BLUE CHEESE DRESSING & SOUR CURRANTS SALAD

## INGREDIENTS

**SERVES 4**

4 heads of baby gem, halved and cored
100g (3½oz/¾ cup) pistachios, crushed in a pestle
 and mortar

**For the dressing:**
125g (4½oz) Stilton or other blue cheese
250ml (9fl oz/1 cup) sour cream
4 tablespoons buttermilk
4 tablespoons moscatel vinegar
½ teaspoon black pepper
sea salt
a squeeze of lemon juice

**For the sour currants:**
125ml (4fl oz/½ cup) moscatel vinegar
4 tablespoons sweet white wine
65g (2¼oz) currants or dried cherries
100g (3½oz/1 cup) pistachios, crushed

1. Make the dressing by putting the Stilton, sour cream, buttermilk, vinegar and pepper into a blender and blitzing to form a purée. Add salt and lemon juice to taste.

2. To make the sour currants or cherries, put all the ingredients into a pan and cook until the currants or cherries plump up – 5 minutes or so.

3. In a large bowl, toss the baby gems with the dressing. Sprinkle over the currants and the crushed pistachios.

## CHANTERELLES, PARMESAN, WALNUTS & PRESERVED LEMON

### INGREDIENTS

**SERVES 4**

50g (1¾oz) unsalted butter
3 garlic cloves, finely chopped
1 sprig of thyme
200g (7oz) chanterelle or girolle mushrooms
2 tablespoons crushed walnuts
1 teaspoon sea salt
1 teaspoon freshly ground black pepper
1 teaspoon smoked paprika
1 tablespoon double (heavy) cream
1 tablespoon finely chopped parsley
1 tablespoon finely chopped preserved lemon

**To serve:**
8 tostadas (see page 14)
a handful of pea shoots
4 tablespoons Parmesan cheese shavings
dried chilli flakes

1. Heat a frying pan on a medium heat and add the butter, garlic and thyme. Once the butter has melted, add the mushrooms and walnuts along with the salt and pepper. Cook the mushrooms for 3–4 minutes, until they absorb the butter and begin to brown. Remove from the heat and stir through the smoked paprika and cream. Mix in the parsley and preserved lemon.

2. Put 2 tostadas on each plate. Add the mushroom mixture and the pea shoots, then scatter the Parmesan shavings over the top. Sprinkle with dried chilli flakes and serve.

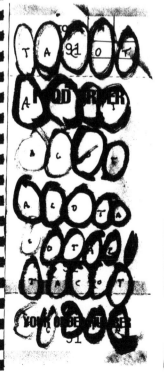

## TRIPLE COOKED PATATAS, RANCHEROS SAUCE & AÏOLI

*You'll need a kitchen thermometer for this recipe, but trust me, you'll end up with the tastiest, crunchiest potatoes.*

### INGREDIENTS

**SERVES 4-6**

500g (1lb 2oz) waxy potatoes
300ml (10fl oz/1¼ cups) olive oil
200ml (7fl oz/scant 1 cup) rancheros sauce (see page 137)
100ml (3½fl oz/scant ½ cup) aïoli (see page 138)
4 tablespoons finely chopped chives
1 jalapeño chilli, finely chopped
1 lime, quartered

1. Quarter the potatoes and cut into 8mm (½ inch) cubes. Place them in a large pot of salted water (as salty as you can stand to sip) and simmer until they are soft in the middle but are still holding their shape. Remove from the heat and drain in a colander.

2. Heat the oil in a heavy-based pan until it reaches 135°C (275°F), then add the drained potatoes and cook for 8 minutes. Remove with a slotted spoon and set aside. (At this stage they can be kept refrigerated for up to 3 days.) When you're ready to eat, heat the oil to 180°C (355°F) and fry the potatoes for 4 minutes – the result will be potatoes that are crunchy on the outside and fluffy in the centre.

3. To serve, put the potatoes on a serving platter and pour over the rancheros sauce. Drizzle some aïoli over the top and sprinkle with the chives and chillies and serve with a spritz of lime.

## CHARCOAL SWEET POTATO WITH MAPLE CHIPOTLE BUTTER & CRÈME FRAÎCHE

*This is a fantastic way of cooking sweet potato, right on the coals of your barbecue. The sweet potato flesh essentially steams in the skin and takes on the lovely charcoal flavour. Served with a chipotle butter, this is a rich, sweet and salty main for a vegetarian or a great side dish for any barbecue.*

### INGREDIENTS

**SERVES 4 AS A SIDE**

500g (1lb 2oz) sweet potatoes
100g (3½oz/½ cup) crème fraîche

**For the maple chipotle butter:**
200g (7oz) butter
100ml (3½fl oz/scant ½ cup) maple syrup
30g (1oz) chipotles in adobo (see page 136)

1. Place the sweet potatoes in the embers of your barbecue and cook for 45 minutes. They're cooked when a sharp knife easily penetrates the skin.

2. Melt the butter in a pan over a low heat and add the maple syrup and chipotles in adobo sauce. Cook for 5 minutes, then set aside.

3. Cut the sweet potatoes in half lengthways. Cross-hatch the flesh with a knife to help the chipotle butter to be absorbed. Drizzle the chipotle butter over the potatoes and finish with the crème fraîche.

## SALT-BAKED VEGETABLES WITH GOAT'S MILK CURDS, HAZELNUTS & MINT OIL

### INGREDIENTS

**SERVES 4**

**For the salt crust:**
3kg (6lb 8oz) fine sea salt
100ml (3½fl oz/scant ½ cup) water
4 egg whites

**For the vegetables:**
4 beetroot (beet), skin on
4 heritage carrots, skin on
2 sweet potatoes, skin on

**To serve:**
200g (7oz) goat's milk curds (see page 139)
100g (3½oz/¾ cup) hazelnuts
100ml (3½fl oz/scant ½ cup) mint oil (see page 134)
sea salt and freshly ground black pepper
8 corn tortillas (see page 16)

1. Preheat the oven to 200°C (400°F/Gas 6). Make the salt crust (following the method on page 84).

2. Wash the vegetables thoroughly and dry. Place on a baking tray and completely cover each vegetable in the salt mixture. Bake in the oven for 40 minutes, then set aside to cool.

3. Once cool, crack the salt crust and remove the vegetables. Split the beetroot and sweet potato and arrange the vegetables on a serving dish. Spoon over the goat's milk curd, scatter over the hazelnuts and drizzle with the mint oil. Season with salt and pepper. Serve with the tortillas.

# BARBECUED WATERMELON, MINT & QUESO FRESCO

*This is best cooked on a barbecue in the heat of summer.*

## INGREDIENTS

**SERVES 4 AS A SNACK**

100ml (3½fl oz/scant ½ cup) agave syrup
juice of 4 limes
1 tablespoon cayenne pepper
1 teaspoon sea salt
1 bird's-eye chilli, very finely chopped
½ teaspoon fish sauce
½ watermelon, cut into 2.5cm (1 inch) wedges

**To serve:**
100g (3½oz) queso fresco (see page 140) or feta cheese
a handful of mint leaves
2 limes, quartered

1. Mix together the agave, lime juice, cayenne, salt, chilli and fish sauce. When your barbecue is hot, brush the watermelon wedges with the mixture and grill for a couple of minutes on each side.

2. Place on a serving plate and sprinkle over the queso fresco and mint leaves. Serve with the lime quarters.

## SPICED CHESTNUT MUSHROOM, PORCINI, TRUFFLE, WALNUTS & BURNT SPRING ONION CREMA

1. In a bowl, mix together the cayenne pepper and smoked paprika, and add a pinch of salt and pepper and a small pinch of sugar. Set aside.

2. Put the dried porcini mushrooms into a bowl or cup and pour boiling water over them, then leave them to brew for 10 minutes.

3. Cut the chestnut mushrooms into slices. Heat the oil in a pan, and when it's hot add chestnut and drained porcini (reserve the liquid) mushrooms and stir and flip to ensure they are coated in the oil. Add the dry spice mix, making sure the mushrooms are well coated in the now flavoured oil. Once the mushrooms have started to cook down and gain colour, add the crushed walnuts and a dash of the porcini soaking juices, as this will add to the intensity. Finish with the truffle oil.

4. Fill your tortillas with the mushroom mix. Add some pico de gallo and a splash of the hot sauce. Add some crema over the top and finally garnish with coriander, radishes and a squeeze of lime.

## INGREDIENTS

### SERVES 4

1 tablespoon cayenne pepper
1 tablespoon smoked paprika
a pinch of sea salt and freshly ground black pepper
a pinch of sugar
20g (¾oz) dried porcini mushrooms
250g (8¾oz/2 cups) chestnut mushrooms
1 tablespoon rapeseed oil
50g (1¾oz/¼ cup) walnuts, crushed
1 teaspoon truffle oil

### To serve:
4 corn tortillas (see page 16)
4 teaspoons pico de gallo (see page 132)
breddos hot sauce (see page 132), to taste
2 tablespoons burnt spring onion crema (see page 138)
finely chopped coriander (cilantro)
4 radishes, sliced
1 lime, quartered

## CAULIFLOWER 'AL PASTOR', PINEAPPLE & PICKLED ONIONS

1. To make the habanero crema, whiz all of the ingredients together in a blender until you have a smooth sauce.

2. In a bowl, whisk together the marinade ingredients until thoroughly combined. Rub the marinade mixture into the cauliflower, being sure to completely cover the two halves. Set aside to marinate for 3–4 hours.

3. Heat your oven to 220°C (425°F/Gas 7). Put the cauliflower halves on a baking tray, cut sides down, and bake in the oven for 1–1½ hours. Take out of the oven, sprinkle the hibiscus powder over the cauliflower and slice into 4cm (1½ inch) segments.

4. Warm up your tortillas and place some of the cauliflower segments on each one. Follow with the habanero crema, ancho chilli oil, pink pickled onions, radishes and pineapple sticks.

## INGREDIENTS

**SERVES 4**

1 head of cauliflower, split in half vertically, cored and trimmed at the base, but with some of the root left on to keep the cauliflower florets together
2 teaspoons ground hibiscus flowers (optional)

**For the marinade:**
100ml (3½fl oz/scant ½ cup) natural yoghurt
100ml (3½fl oz/scant ½ cup) 'al pastor' marinade (see page 97)
1 teaspoon sea salt
1 teaspoon crushed black pepper

**For the habanero crema:**
200ml (7fl oz/scant 1 cup) crema (see page 140) or sour cream
2 chipotles in adobo (see page 136)
1 dried habanero chilli, soaked in hot water for 30 minutes
1 teaspoon dried oregano

**To serve:**
8 corn tortillas (see page 16)
½ teaspoon ancho chilli oil (see page 134), or to taste
pink pickled onions (see page 53)
4 radishes, halved
½ pineapple, sliced into sticks, roasted in a dry frying pan or chargrill pan until blackened

## CHARRED CORN, HABANERO MAYONNAISE & QUESO FRESCO

*My earliest memory of eating corn was when I was very young, living in Zambia. Every day on the way home from school I used to stop at the corner of my road and buy corn from an old lady who sat there all day, barbecuing the cobs on a tiny stove. She'd serve the corn very simply, with just a sprinkle of salt.*

*In later years, when travelling through Mexico, I came across similar old ladies, selling pimped-up corn, Mexican style. This recipe is based on those Mexican corns I came across. Of course, if you'd like to cook them the Zambian way, just omit all the extra ingredients!*

1. Peel back the husks on the corn and tie them into a knot. This not only looks great but also gives you something to hold onto during both preparation and eating. Fill a deep saucepan with enough water to submerge the corn. Add salt and bring to the boil. Once boiling, add the corn and boil for around 8 minutes, until it softens and turns a vivid yellow, then drain.

2. On a tray or large plate, mix the grated Parmesan with the smoked paprika and chipotle powder.

3. Heat a griddle pan and add your corn – you're looking to add colour to it all around.

4. Once your corn is browned, smear it in the butter and add a sprinkling of salt. Rub the habanero mayonnaise into the corn; it's then ready to roll in the cheese and paprika mix. Make sure that you give it a liberal coating, the heat of the corn will turn it into a delicious oozing mess. Sprinkle with the lime zest and squeeze over the lime juice before swirling over the crema.

## INGREDIENTS

### SERVES 4

4 corn on the cobs (husks left on)
sea salt
100g (3½oz) Parmesan cheese, finely grated
2 teaspoons smoked paprika
1 teaspoon chipotle powder
2 tablespoons butter
100ml (3½fl oz/½ cup) habanero
  aïoli (see page 138)
200g (7oz) queso fresco (see page 140)
  or feta cheese
1 lime, zest and juice
200ml (7fl oz/scant 1 cup) crema (see page 140)
  or sour cream

# DRINKS

# AGUAS FRESCAS

*Mexicans also do juice, but in their own special way. Below are a selection of our favourites, but feel free to experiment with your own fruit combinations.*

## SUGAR SYRUP

100ml (3½fl oz/scant ½ cup) water
85g (3oz) caster (superfine) sugar

1. Place sugar and water in a pot and cook until dissolved.

## 1. BLACKBERRY & LEMON

### INGREDIENTS

**Makes 300ml (10fl oz/1¼ cups)**

2 punnets of blackberries
juice of 8 lemons
100ml (3½fl oz/scant ½ cup) sugar syrup (above)

1. Reserve a few of the blackberries for serving. Blitz everything together and serve over ice with some blackberries added to the top.

## 2. WATERMELON & MINT

### INGREDIENTS

**Makes 500ml (17fl oz/2½ cups)**

a bunch of mint, leaves picked
60ml (2fl oz/¼ cup) sugar syrup (above)
1.5kg (3lb 5oz) watermelon, deseeded and cubed
juice of 8 limes

1. Place the mint and sugar syrup in a pan and cook on a medium heat until simmering. Strain through a sieve, cool, then pour into a blender jug and add the watermelon and lime juice. Blitz and serve over ice.

## 3. PASSION FRUIT, PINEAPPLE & LIME

### INGREDIENTS

**Makes 250ml (8½fl oz/1¼ cups)**

10 passion fruit, split in half, pulp scooped out
50ml (2fl oz/¼ cup) sugar syrup (above)
juice of 5 limes
100ml (3½fl oz/scant ½ cup) pineapple juice

1. Blend all the ingredients together and serve over ice.

## 4. MANGO & COCONUT

### INGREDIENTS

**Makes 350ml (12fl oz/scant 1½ cups)**

5 Alphonso mangos, cored and peeled
100ml (3½fl oz/scant ½ cup) coconut water
juice of 2 limes
50ml (2fl oz/¼ cup) sparkling water

1. Blend all the ingredients and serve in a glass, topping up with sparkling water

## CHILLIBACK

### INGREDIENTS

**Makes for one drunk taco vendor**

1 shot of blanco tequila
1 shot of the chilliback juice (see pickled habaneros,
    pages 132–3)

1. Shoot the tequila, chase with chilliback juice.

# SALSAS & CONDIMENTS

*Breddos Tacos uses salsas in the same way that Mexicans do – as an accompaniment to pretty much everything we make. They are my go-to staples in the kitchen, adding depth, spice, acidity, umami or just raw chilli heat, depending on which I decide to use. When we started out in the shack, we probably had only three or four salsas in our arsenal. A couple of years on, and many dishes later, we probably have over 50. There's no hard and fast rule to flavour matching these salsas, just go ahead and experimentally mix and match salsas with your dishes. As our friend Bill Esparza in L.A. says, 'You are the sous chef to your taco', i.e. simply garnish away until you find your happy place!*

*Most of these salsas will last between 3–5 days in the refrigerator if stored in a sterilized jar.*

## PICO DE GALLO | Makes 400g (14oz/scant 2 cups)

300g (11oz) ripe vine tomatoes
2 medium red onions, diced
½ bunch of coriander (cilantro), finely chopped
½ jalapeño chilli, deseeded and finely chopped
1 teaspoon sea salt
1 teaspoon freshly ground black pepper
1 teaspoon sugar
juice of 2–3 limes
1 teaspoon rapeseed oil

1. First quarter the tomatoes. Remove the cores, then dice the tomatoes into 5mm (¼ inch) cubes and put them into a large bowl.

2. Add the diced red onions to the bowl with the coriander and jalapeños. Add salt and pepper and taste to check the seasoning

3. Once you're happy with the flavour, mix in the sugar. Add lime juice, to taste, and the oil. Stir to combine and taste again – the mixture should be salty, sweet, zingy and slightly spicy. If you like your salsas hot, replace the jalapeño with a Scotch bonnet or habanero.

## BREDDOS HOT SAUCE
## Makes 400ml (14fl oz/scant 2 cups)

*We highly recommend wearing silicone kitchen gloves when making this recipe.*

2–3 Scotch bonnet chillies
small pinch of sea salt
2 large tablespoons sugar
juice of 4 limes

1½ x 400g (14oz) tins of peeled plum tomatoes
a handful of coriander (cilantro), chopped

1. Remove the stalks and quarter the Scotch bonnets. If you want to reduce the heat of the sauce, remove the seeds at this stage. Put the Scotch bonnets into a blender and blitz.

2. Add the salt and sugar and squeeze in the lime juice. Blitz again for a moment. Add the tomatoes and coriander and blitz again.

3. The tomato taste should fall into the background, with sweet citrus flavours coming through and building, with quite a long-lasting heat.

## SALTED CHILLI PASTE | Makes 100g (3½oz/¼ cup)

15 long red chillies
5 bird's-eye chillies
2 tablespoons sea salt
5 garlic cloves
1 tablespoon apple cider vinegar

1. Pulse all the ingredients in a blender until you have a rough paste. Place in a sterilized glass jar and seal. Stir daily for a week, after which the paste will be slightly fermented and ready to use.

## CASCABEL CHILLI SALT | Makes 50g (1¾oz/¼ cup)

6 dried cascabel chillies
3 tablespoons sea salt
1 teaspoon smoked paprika

1. Toast the chillies in a frying pan over a medium heat for a couple of minutes.

2. Once cool, put into a spice grinder or pestle and mortar and grind to a fine powder. Mix in the salt and smoked paprika.

## PICKLED HABANEROS | Makes 100g (3½oz/½ cup)

200ml (7fl oz/scant 1 cup) apple cider vinegar
2 tablespoons sugar
1½ teaspoons Maldon sea salt
100g (3½oz) habanero chillies
1 tablespoon mustard seeds

1. Bring the cider vinegar to a simmer in a pan and mix in the sugar and salt. While this is simmering, slice the

habaneros into concentric rings. You can remove the seeds to decrease the heat, though they'll still be very hot. Place the chillies in a Mason or pickling jar (or just an old jam jar) and pour over the vinegar mix. Leave to pickle for a few days before using.

## X NI PEK (MAYAN SALSA)
### Makes 400g (14oz/scant 2 cups)

*X ni pek literally means hot as a dog's nose, and is all about curing red onions in citrus, which effectively cuts through the richness of the cochinita pibil pork.*

3 red onions, very finely sliced and soaked in
 ice-cold water for 10 minutes
5 tablespoons freshly squeezed orange juice
1 tablespoon grapefruit juice
juice of 4 limes
½ habanero, deseeded, deveined and finely chopped

1. Drain the onions and put in a bowl. Pour over the orange, grapefruit and lime juices and add the chilli. Leave the onions to 'cook' in the citric acid for about an hour. They're ready when they turn a vivid pink colour.

## GUACAMOLE | Makes 400g (14oz/scant 2 cups)

*We use this guacamole as the base for a number of sauces in our kitchen, and the purity of the recipe relies on your sourcing the best, ripest avocados you can find. If you're preparing the guacamole in advance, put the stones back into the avocado mix – this will prevent oxidization.*

4 or 5 jalapeño chillies
½ bunch of coriander (cilantro)
6 ripe avocados
1 tablespoon rapeseed oil
sea salt and freshly ground black pepper
juice of 3 limes

1. Deseed the jalapeños, then very finely chop them and the coriander.

2. Slice your avocados through the middle and split. Take out the stones and set aside (they'll be useful later). Scoop out the flesh of the avocado and place on a chopping board and add the oil. Taking a fork, mash the avocados into a rough paste, making sure you retain a decent amount of texture. Throw the chopped chillies and coriander into the mix and season. Fold all the ingredients together using the fork, ensuring that they're evenly distributed. Once you've done this, squeeze the lime juice over the top and mix through.

## AVOCADO MOJO | Makes 300ml (10fl oz/1¼ cups)

1 quantity of guacamole (see above)
3 garlic cloves, finely chopped
1 tablespoon roasted garlic oil (see page 134)
1 jalapeño chilli
1 teaspoon dried oregano
juice of 1 lime
a handful of coriander (cilantro)
1 teaspoon chilli flakes
sea salt and freshly ground black pepper

1. Place all the ingredients in a blender and pulse. You may need to scrape down the sides of the jug and add some water if the mojo is too thick.

## AVOCADO HOT SAUCE
### Makes 150ml (5fl oz/generous ½ cup)

100ml (3½fl oz/scant ½ cup) avocado mojo (see above)
2 jalapeño chillies
2 tablespoons sour cream
juice of 2 limes
1 habanero or Scotch bonnet chilli

1. Place all the ingredients in a blender and pulse until you have a smooth sauce.

## CHIPOTLE KETCHUP | Makes 300ml (10fl oz/1¼ cups)

200ml (7fl oz/scant 1 cup) tomato ketchup
100g (3½oz/scant ½ cup) chipotles in adobo
 (see page 136)

1. Simply blend together in a ratio of two parts ketchup to one part chipotle. (You can adjust to your own tastes but we find that these proportions give the best results.)

## RUSSIAN DRESSING | Makes 200ml (7fl oz/1 cup)

100ml (3½fl oz/scant ½ cup) ketchup
100ml (3½fl oz/scant ½ cup) mayonnaise
a pinch each of sea salt and freshly ground black pepper
50g (1¾oz) cornichons, finely chopped
2 jalapeño chillies, deseeded and finely chopped
a dash of Worcestershire sauce
juice of 1 lime

1. In a bowl, mix together the ketchup, mayonnaise and salt and pepper.

2. Fold the cornichons and jalapeños into the mix, making

sure they are distributed evenly – alternatively you can use a blender to do this.

3. Add the Worcestershire sauce and, to add some zing, the lime juice.

## CHIPOTLE CASHEW NUT SALSA
### Makes around 300g (11oz/1½ cups)

200g (7oz/1¾ cups) salted cashew nuts
4 tablespoons chipotles in adobo (see page 136)
4 tablespoons water
juice of 1 lime

1. Roast the cashews in a dry pan until aromatic, for about 2 minutes.

2. Put all the ingredients into a blender and pulse until you have a rough salsa with the consistency of wholegrain mustard. You're looking for a smoky and spicy flavour. Store in an airtight jar for up to 2 weeks.

# FLAVOURED OILS

## CORIANDER OIL | Makes 400ml (14fl oz/1¾ cups)

200g (7oz) coriander (cilantro) leaves
400ml (14fl oz/1¾ cups) olive oil

1. Fill a bowl with ice-cold water. Bring some water to the boil in a small pan and drop in the coriander leaves. Blanch for 5 seconds, then drain and place immediately in the ice-cold water.

2. Once the leaves are cool, after about 5 minutes, squeeze them dry and place them in a pan with the olive oil. Cook over a medium heat until the oil starts to bubble very slightly or reaches 60°C (140°F). Take off the heat and let cool, then strain into a blender and whizz on high speed. Store in a dark place to ensure the oil keeps its colour.

## THYME OIL | Makes 200ml (7fl oz/1 cup)

200ml (7fl oz/1 cup) extra-virgin olive or rapeseed oil
4 sprigs thyme, washed and dried
peel of ½ lemon

1. Bruise the herbs by whacking them on a table a few times.

2. Heat the olive oil and thyme in a saucepan until small bubbles form on the surface of the oil. Allow to cool, add the lemon peel and transfer to a sterilized jar.

## MINT OIL | Makes 400ml (13½fl oz/1¾ cups)

200g (7oz) mint leaves
400ml (14fl oz/1¾ cups) olive oil

1. Follow the same instructions as for the coriander oil, above.

## OREGANO, CHILLI & GARLIC OIL
### Makes about 1 litre (1¾ pints/4 cups)

3 heads of garlic, halved horizontally
10 árbol chillies
3 guajillo chillies
a bunch of oregano
1 litre (1¾ pints/4 cups) olive oil

1. Put all the ingredients into a pan and cook over a medium heat until you see bubbles forming. Turn the heat down and continue to cook for a further 20 minutes. Remove from the heat and leave to steep for 2 hours.

2. Strain the oil through a fine sieve into a bottle, pressing down on all the solids to extract their flavour.

## ANCHO CHILLI OIL
### Makes about 1 litre (1¾ pints/4 cups)

5 garlic cloves
20 ancho chillies
4 sprigs of rosemary
2 sprigs of thyme
1 litre (1¾ pints/4 cups) olive oil

1. Put all the ingredients into a pan and cook over a medium heat until you see bubbles forming. Turn the heat down and continue to cook for a further 20 minutes. Remove from the heat and leave to steep for 2 hours.

2. Strain the oil through a fine sieve into a bottle, pressing down on all the solids to extract their flavour.

## ROASTED GARLIC OIL
### Makes about 400ml (14oz/1¾ cups)

3 heads of garlic, cloves, separated and peeled
1 sprig of thyme
1 sprig of rosemary
400ml (14fl oz/1¾ cups) olive oil

1. Toast the garlic in a dry frying pan until blackened. Add the thyme, rosemary and oil and cook on a very low heat for 30 minutes. Remove from the heat and cool. Store in an airtight container.

## CHERMOULA | Makes about 400ml (14oz/1¾ cups)

100ml (3½fl oz/scant ½ cup) coriander (cilantro) oil (see page 134)
100ml (3½fl oz/scant ½ cup) mint oil (see page 134)
1 Scotch bonnet chilli, deseeded and deveined
100g (3½oz) parsley leaves
50g (1¾oz) coriander (cilantro) leaves
50g (1¾oz) mint leaves
1 teaspoon toasted cumin seeds
2 garlic cloves, peeled and smashed
3cm (1¼ inch) piece of peeled ginger, roughly chopped
a pinch of sea salt
juice of 2 limes

1. Place all the ingredients in a blender and blitz on high speed until combined.

## MANGO, LIME & HABANERO SALSA
## Makes 200g (7oz/1 cup)

1 mango, cut into small cubes
juice of 2 limes
1 habanero chilli
a handful of coriander (cilantro) leaves, chopped
a handful of mint leaves, chopped
a pinch of sea salt
a pinch of sugar
1 teaspoon olive oil

1. Mix all the ingredients together and store in the fridge until needed.

## TOMATILLO SALSA | Makes 800g (1lb 12oz/4 cups)

*If you want to ramp up the smokiness in this dish, roast the tomatillos in a dry pan until blackened, then blend.*

2 jalapeño chillies, roughly chopped
2 large garlic cloves, peeled and crushed
1kg (2lb 3oz) fresh tomatillos, husked, washed and sliced in half
1 shallot
½ avocado, stoned and diced
2 tablespoons coriander (cilantro) leaves, chopped
juice of 1 lime
½ teaspoon sea salt
1. Place the jalapeños, garlic, tomatillos and shallot in a blender and pulse until smooth. Add the avocado and some water if the mixture is too thick. Fold in the coriander, lime juice and salt.

## JALAPEÑO & ACHIOTE BUTTER | Makes 55g (2oz/¼ cup)

50g (1¾oz) butter, at room temperature
1 teaspoon achiote paste
2 jalapeño chillies, very finely diced

1. Put the butter into a bowl and add the achiote paste. Mix the two together, then add the diced jalapeños and combine. Take a 30cm (12 inch) square of clingfilm (plastic wrap) and spoon the butter into the middle. Roll the right and left edges of the clingfilm towards each other to create a cylindrical tube within which the butter resides. Place in the fridge until you're ready to use.

## JALAPEÑO & APPLE RELISH | Makes 250g (US CUPS)

5 jalapeño chillies
1 shallot, roughly chopped
1 small apple, roughly chopped
1 tablespoon agave syrup
3 tablespoons chopped coriander (cilantro) leaves
½ teaspoon sea salt

1. Put all the ingredients into a blender and whizz on high speed for 1 minute. Scrape down the sides of the jug and whizz again until you have a chunky sauce. Depending on how sweet or sour you like your salsa, you may want to add more agave or salt.

## SHACK SALSA VERDE | Makes 400g (14oz/2 cups)

75g (3oz) parsley, chopped
25g (1oz) coriander (cilantro), chopped
1 tablespoon roughly chopped garlic
100g (3½oz) spring onions (scallions), chopped
1 bunch of fresh thyme, chopped
125ml (4fl oz/½ cup) water
2 teaspoons grated lime zest
6 tablespoons fresh lime juice
1 Scotch bonnet chilli, cut in half and deseeded
1 tablespoon sea salt
1 tablespoon fresh peeled and chopped ginger
375ml (13fl oz/1½ cups) olive oil

1. Place all the ingredients apart from the olive oil in a blender and pulse on high. Reduce the speed and slowly add the olive oil until emulsified.

## SALSA ROJA | Makes 200ml (7fl oz/scant 1 cup)

15 árbol chillies
2 guajillo or ancho chillies
3 garlic cloves, unpeeled
3 tomatoes
1 tablespoon red wine vinegar
a pinch of sea salt
lard (optional)

1. Toast the chillies, garlic and tomatoes in a dry pan until fragrant – for the chillies, this should take 30–45 seconds, after which they need to be deseeded and submerged in hot water. The garlic and tomatoes can be left in the pan until their skins blister and turn black, about 4–5 minutes.

2. Put the chillies into a blender with a few tablespoons of their soaking water and pulse. Peel the garlic cloves and add to the blender along with the vinegar, tomatoes and salt. Pulse until you have a smooth sauce.

3. You can decant and store it at this point, or take the recipe one stage further by heating some lard in a stockpot until smoking hot and adding the salsa to the pot – it will splutter and spit, so be careful, but by doing this you're essentially cooking out the raw ingredients, which will give your salsa a rounder and deeper flavour.

## ADOBO | Makes 200g (7oz/1 cup)

6 ancho chillies, deseeded and deveined
6 guajillo chillies, deseeded and deveined
75g (3oz) canned chipotle chillies
4 garlic cloves, roasted
250ml (9fl oz/1 cup) cider vinegar
½ teaspoon Mexican oregano
1 teaspoon black peppercorns
½ teaspoon cumin seeds, toasted
½ teaspoon cloves, toasted
1cm (½ inch) stick of cinnamon, ½ teaspoon ground
  cinnamon powder

1. In a non-stick pan over a high flame, toast the ancho and guajillo chillies until they begin to blister, then soak them in warm water for about 25 minutes, until soft and malleable.

2. Remove the chillies and discard the soaking water. Put the soaked chillies into a blender with the remaining ingredients and purée until smooth. Transfer the mixture to a bowl and stir thoroughly with a rubber spatula. Keep refrigerated.

## HABANERO/SCOTCH BONNET SALSA
Makes 200ml (7fl oz/scant 1 cup)

10 habanero or Scotch bonnet chillies, destemmed and
  deseeded
1 tablespoon olive oil
1 white onion, chopped
100ml (3½fl oz/scant ½ cup) orange juice
1 teaspoon grated orange zest
1 tablespoon lime juice and 1 teaspoon grated lime zest
75ml (3fl oz/scant ⅓ cup) cider vinegar
a pinch of Mexican oregano
3½ tablespoons sugar
75ml (3fl oz/scant ⅓ cup) water
1 tablespoon sea salt

1. Toast the chillies in a dry pan until blackened. Remove and set aside. Heat the oil in the same pan and add the onion. Fry over a low heat until soft, about 7 minutes.

2. Put all the ingredients into a blender or food processor and blend to a coarse purée. Transfer the mixture to a saucepan over a low heat and simmer gently for 30 minutes. Remove the salsa from the heat and let cool to room temperature. Store in the fridge in an airtight container.

## SALSA DE ÁRBOL | Makes 400g (14oz/2 cups)

40g (1½oz) árbol chillies, destemmed and deseeded
2 tablespoons extra virgin olive oil
1 teaspoon allspice
½ teaspoon ground cumin
40g (1½oz) sesame seeds
40g (1½oz) pumpkin seeds
40g (1½oz) sugar
20g (¾oz) sea salt
300ml (11fl oz/1¼ cups) cider vinegar
300ml (11fl oz/1¼ cups) water

1. Soak the árbol chillies in hot water in a metal or heatproof bowl for 1 hour.

2. Meanwhile, toast the spices In a dry pan over a low to medium heat, making sure they do not burn. Remove and set aside. Heat the olive oil in the same pan and fry the sesame seeds and pumpkin seeds in separate batches. Transfer to a plate and set aside.

2. Drain the chillies, discarding the soaking liquid. Return to the heatproof bowl and add the toasted spices and fried seeds.

3. In a pan, bring the sugar, salt, cider vinegar and water to the boil. Pour over the chilli mixture and let it cool to room temperature, then transfer to a blender and purée until smooth. Transfer to a container with an airtight lid.

## LECHE DE TIGRE (TIGER'S MILK)
### Makes 50ml (1¾fl oz/¼ cup)

5mm (¼ inch) piece of peeled ginger, cut in half
1 small garlic clove
4 sprigs of coriander (cilantro), roughly chopped
juice of 8 limes
2 teaspoons salsa roja (see page 136) or chilli paste
½ teaspoon sea salt

1. Combine everything apart from the salsa roja in a bowl and stir to infuse. Strain into a second bowl and add the salt. Stir in the salsa roja and mix well.

## RANCHERAS SAUCE | Makes 500ml (17fl oz/2¼ cups)

2 tablespoons rapeseed oil
1 onion, finely chopped
2 garlic cloves, crushed
2 long red chillies, finely chopped
1 jalapeño chilli, finely chopped
1 x 400g (14oz) tin of chopped tomatoes
2 chipotles in adobo, with 1 teaspoon of the sauce
1 teaspoon cayenne
1 teaspoon sugar
1 teaspoon sea salt
1 teaspoon smoked paprika
1–2 tablespoons sherry or moscatel vinegar

1. Put the oil into a heavy-based pan on a medium heat, and cook the onion for about 7 minutes, until golden and soft. Add the garlic and chillies and cook for another couple of minutes, then add the tomatoes, chipotles, cayenne, sugar, salt and smoked paprika and stir well. Bring to the boil, then turn down the heat and simmer for about 30 minutes until thick and dark and you can see a film of oil on the surface of the tomatoes.

2. Take off the heat, add 1 tablespoon of vinegar, adding more and adjusting the seasoning if necessary.

## SESAME SEED & PUMPKIN SEED SALSA
### Makes 400g (14oz/2 cups)

200g (7oz/1½ cups) sesame seeds
200g (7oz/1½ cups) pumpkin seeds
100g (3½oz/¾ cup) skinless, blanched almonds
2 tablespoons chipotles in adobo (see page 136)
juice of 2 limes
sea salt and freshly ground black pepper
1 tablespoon rapeseed oil
100ml (3½fl oz/scant ½ cup) tepid water

1. Toast the sesame and pumpkin seeds in a pan for 30 seconds, then add the almonds for another 30 seconds.

2. Put all the ingredients into a blender apart from the water, and pulse. Add enough water to loosen the mixture, until you have the consistency of wholegrain mustard.

## PEA MOLE | Makes 300ml (10fl oz/1¼ cups)

150g (1¼ cups) frozen peas
50g (1¾oz/⅓ cup) sesame seeds
50g (1¾oz/½ cup) skinned almonds
3 tablespoons pumpkin seeds
juice of 2 limes
handful of mint leaves, finely chopped
½ teaspoon chilli flakes
½ teaspoon each of salt and pepper
1 garlic clove, finely chopped.

1. Cook the peas in boiling water for 2 minutes, then transfer straight into a bowl of ice-cold water. This will retain their bright green hue.

2. Toast the sesame seeds, almonds and pumpkin seeds in a dry frying pan for 2 minutes. Remove from the heat.

3. Put the toasted seeds and remaining ingredients in a blender. Add the drained peas and pulse for 1 minute, until you have a smooth velvety sauce. If you want to get cheffy you can pass this sauce through a fine mesh strainer to remove any bits. Serve immediately.

## BLACK MOLE | Makes 500g (17½oz/2½ cups)

25g (1oz) dried oregano
50g (1¾oz) cayenne pepper
50g (1¾oz) smoked paprika
1 stick of cinnamon
50g (1¾oz/⅓ cup) almonds
50g (1¾oz/⅓ cup) pecans
50g (1¾oz/½ cup) pumpkin seeds
50g (1¾oz) garlic cloves, unpeeled
50g (1¾oz) árbol chillies, roasted and soaked
  in water for 30 minutes
3 corn tortillas (see page 16), torn up
50g (1¾oz) guajillo chillies, dry roasted and soaked
  in water for 30 minutes
50g (1¾oz/⅓ cup) raisins
½ banana, peeled
50g (1¾oz) good-quality dark chocolate (min. 70% cocoa
  solids) or 3 tablespoons cocoa powder
100ml (3½fl oz/scant ½ cup) water
100ml (3½fl oz/scant ½ cup) beef stock, reduced to 50ml
  (2fl oz/¼ cup) on a low heat for 30 minutes
25g (1oz) freshly ground black pepper
3 tablespoons lard or butter

*Traditional mole recipes are defined by processes and*

levels of complexity – they involve toasting, burning, frying, blending and sieving. This is not a traditional mole recipe. It's a quick adaptation to allow you to incorporate great flavour into a dish without too much complexity and time. You only need one pan and one blender for this recipe, and it's worth making at least once.

1. Toast all your herbs, spices, nuts and seeds in a dry pan for a few minutes until fragrant. Remove and set aside. Add the garlic to the same pan and toast until the skin is burnt and blistered – 10 minutes. Remove and set aside. Add the torn-up tortillas to the pan and toast until black.

2. Put all the ingredients apart from the lard or butter into a blender and pulse. Scrape down the sides of the blender and add some water if the sauce is really thick.

3. Heat up the pan you were using for the spices until scorching hot. Add the lard or butter and let it melt. Being very careful, add the blender contents to the pan – it should fizz and spit. Lower the heat and let the sauce cook down for 10 minutes. If it's a little too thick, add water. Once it's done, decant into a jar and keep for up to 2 weeks.

## AÏOLI | Makes 250g (8¾oz/1¼ cups)

2 small garlic cloves, peeled
sea salt and freshly ground black pepper
2 large free-range egg yolks
½ teaspoon English or Dijon mustard
1 teaspoon white wine vinegar
250ml (9fl oz/1 cup) sunflower or rapeseed oil

1. Crush the garlic to a paste with a pinch of sea salt, then thoroughly combine in a bowl with the egg yolks, mustard, vinegar and some pepper. In a slow steady stream, whisk the oil into the egg mix, a few drops at a time to start with, then in small dashes, whisking in each addition so it is properly emulsified before adding the next. By the time you've added all the oil, you should have a thick, glossy, wobbly aïoli that holds its shape.

2. Taste and add more salt, pepper, mustard or vinegar if you like. If it seems too thick, stir in a tablespoon or two of warm water to let it down.

## HABANERO AÏOLI | Makes 250g (8¾oz/1¼ cups)

5 dried habanero chillies, soaked in hot water to soften
1 teaspoon Mexican oregano
1 quantity aïoli (see above)

1. Blend the habaneros and oregano in a food processor or blender until you have a smooth paste. Add the aïoli and blend again until incorporated.

## LIME AÏOLI | Makes 250g (8¾oz/1¼ cups)

Substitute 1 tablespoon lime juice for the cider vinegar in the aïoli recipe (see above).

## JALAPEÑO MAYONNAISE | Makes 250g (8¾oz/1¼ cups)

2 fresh jalapeño chillies, roughly chopped
1 teaspoon sea salt
1 quantity aïoli (see above), omitting the garlic

1. Blend the jalapeños with the salt until a paste forms. Add the aïoli and blend until incorporated.

## CHIPOTLE MAYONNAISE | Makes 275g (9¾oz/scant 1½ cups)

2 chipotles in adobo, with 2 tablespoons sauce
1 tablespoon water
1 quantity aïoli (see page above), omitting the garlic

1. Blend the chipotles with the water and the adobo sauce until a smooth paste forms. Add the aïoli and blitz on high speed until incorporated.

## CHIPOTLE CREMA | Makes 225ml (8fl oz/generous 1 cup)

1 quantity crema (see page 140)
2 chipotles in adobo, with 1 teaspoon sauce
1 garlic clove
1 teaspoon Mexican oregano
sea salt and freshly ground black pepper

1. Place all the ingredients in a blender and pulse until smooth and combined. Taste to check the seasoning.

## BURNT SPRING ONION (SCALLION) CREMA Makes 250ml (8fl oz/generous 1 cup)

2 bunches spring onions (scallions)
200ml (7fl oz/1 cup) crema (see page 140) or sour cream

1. Clean the spring onions and trim the root and tips. Use a griddle pan, or better still a barbecue, and get it nice and hot. If using a griddle pan, wipe the surface with some plain cooking oil (rapeseed works well), and place the spring onions on a medium to high heat. Let the onions sit so that they get nicely blackened, turning them from time to time.

2. Once the onions are ready, blitz them with the crema or sour cream and you'll have a lovely complement to some of our more savoury tacos, such as the short-rib or the mushroom.

## SMOKY STEAK MARINADE
**Makes 300ml (11oz/1½ cups)**

1 head of garlic, cloves separated and peeled
¼ onion, peeled
3–4 spring onions (scallions), chopped
2 tablespoons chipotle chilli powder or
   smoked paprika
3 chipotles in adobo (see page 136)
1 tablespoon freshly ground black pepper
2 jalapeño chillies
½ bunch of coriander (cilantro)
180ml (6fl oz/¾ cup) beer
juice and grated zest of 1 orange
juice and grated zest of 1 grapefruit
juice and grated zest of 3 limes
1 tablespoon each of sea salt and freshly ground
   black pepper
1 tablespoon sugar
2 tablespoons rapeseed or groundnut oil

1. Put everything in a blender and blitz to a paste.


## HABANERO MIGNONETTE FOR OYSTERS
**Makes 50ml (1¾fl oz/¼ cup)**

1 habanero chilli
1 medium tomato, deseeded and finely diced
1 medium shallot, finely diced
2 tablespoons finely chopped coriander (cilantro)
2 tablespoons fresh lime juice
1 teaspoon fish sauce
fine sea salt, to taste
1 teaspoon agave syrup

1. Roast the habanero in a dry pan until blackened and blistered, then deseed and finely chop.

2. Fold together the habanero chilli, tomato, shallot, coriander, lime juice, fish sauce and sea salt in a small bowl, then stir in the agave.


# HOW TO

### DEVEIN A CHILLI

Cut along the length of the chilli. Scoop out the seeds using a teaspoon. Remove the white veins with a paring knife.

### BRINE

To create 10% salt water brine, dissolve 100g (3½oz/½ cup) of salt per 1 litre (1¾ pints/4 cups) water.

### ROAST CHILLIES

Heat a dry pan on medium heat until hot, about 5 minutes. Put the chillies in the pan and toast until very aromatic, about 1 minute per side - the chillies will intensify in colour.

### SPATCHCOCK A CHICKEN

1. Put the chicken breast-side down with the legs pointing towards you. Using kitchen shears, cut along the right side of the backbone, then along the left side.

2. Remove the backbone and keep for stock. Flatten the chicken by flipping the chicken over and pushing down on the breast bone.

### MAKE GLUTINOUS RICE POWDER

Toast the glutinous rice in a dry frying pan over a medium heat for 5-6 minutes, until the rice has turned a darker colour and released a nutty odour, reminiscent of popcorn. Put the rice in the pestle and mortar and pound to a fine powder. This should last for up to 3 months.

### MAKE GOAT'S MILK CURDS
**Makes about 400g (14fl oz/scant 2 cups)**

1 litre (1¾ pints/4 cups) full-fat goat's milk
   (pasteurized works fine)
1 tablespoon rennet
2 tablespoons lemon juice
salt

1. Heat the milk to 25°C (77°F) and take off the heat. Stir in the rennet and lemon juice, then cover the pan and leave to rest for an hour. Line a colander with muslin (cheesecloth) and stand it over a large bowl. Strain the mixture through the muslin. Gather the corners of the cloth and hang it over a bowl. Leave to drip for a couple of hours until the consistency of the cheese seems right to you.

## MAKE QUESO FRESCO | Makes 800g (1lb 12oz/4 cups)

4 litres (7 pints/4 quarts) whole/raw milk
200ml (7fl oz/scant 1 cup) fresh lemon juice
1 tablespoon sea salt

1. Line a colander with 4 sheets muslin (cheesecloth) and place over a pan. In another pan, heat the milk to 80°C (176°F), then remove from the heat and add the salt. Add the lemon juice 1 tablespoon at a time, stopping when the curds (white solids) separate from the whey (the liquid).

2. Let the mixture stand for 20 minutes. Using a slotted spoon, take the curds out of the pan and place in the colander. Fold over the muslin and weight down with a heavy pot for a couple of hours until you have a condensed cheese. Refrigerate until needed.

## MAKE HOMEMADE CREMA
## Makes 250ml (8¾oz/1¼ cups)

*Crema is a kind of Mexican sour cream/crème fraîche hybrid. It's not difficult to make and the taste is far superior to anything you'll get from normal sour cream or crème fraîche.*

200ml (7fl oz/scant 1 cup) organic double (heavy) cream
1½ tablespoons organic buttermilk

1. Heat the double cream in a pan to 35°C (95°F), take off the heat and pour into a glass jar. Add the buttermilk, place the lid on the jar loosely and store in a jar in a warm place for 24 hours. Then tighten the lid and store in the fridge.

## MAKE REFRIED BEANS | Makes 400g (14oz/2 cups)

400g (14oz/2 cups) dried pinto beans or 1 tin of canned
   pinto beans
1 large onion, diced
3 cloves garlic, toasted with their skins on until black spots appear, then peeled and minced
1 teaspoon epazote
1 teaspoon Mexican oregano
1 teaspoon ground coriander
1 teaspoon ground cumin
1 teaspoon chipotle powder
1 tablespoon Maldon salt
4 tablespoons lard or rapeseed oil, plus
   2 more tablespoons

1. Wash the beans under running cold water, if using dried beans.

2. Take a medium-sized pot, add the lard or rapeseed oil and heat. Add the onions and cook over a gentle heat, stirring often, until translucent, about 10 minutes.

3. Add the garlic, oregano, epazote, coriander, cumin, chipotle and salt and cook for another 3 minutes, then add the pinto beans and after a minute, cover with water (if using dried beans).

4. If using canned beans, cook for another 10 minutes and go to step 6.

5. Bring to a boil then reduce to a high simmer and cook the beans until very soft, around 1-2 hours. Drain, reserving a cup of the liquid.

6. Place the beans in a blender and whizz to a paste.

7. Heat the 2 extra tablespoons of lard or rapeseed oil in another pot and once hot, add the beans. Re-fry for 3-4 minutes adding some of the reserved bean cooking liquid if too thick.

## MAKE TOMATO CONFIT | Makes 200g (7oz/1 cup)

500g (1lb) cherry tomatoes
2 garlic cloves, minced
2 teaspoons fresh thyme
100ml (3½fl oz/½ cup) olive oil
1 teaspoon Maldon sea salt

1. Preheat the oven to 100ºC (212°F).

2. Slice the tomatoes in half horizontally and place in a roasting dish with all of the other ingredients

3. Cook in the oven for 2 hours, turning once after an hour.

# INDEX

## ACKNOWLEDGEMENTS

There are too many people that we've met along the way, who have helped us in one way or another to mention here, but we'd especially like to thank:

Annette and Jess for being the most understanding loving partners, putting up with our incessant strategizing and phone calls and most of all for allowing us to go to America and Mexico every year (forever?).

Our parents for all of the support they've shown to two kids who dropped out of great jobs to stand in a car park and sell tacos.

JD for being an incredible breddo, our fairy godfather and, ultimately, showing us the way to the vibes.

Gringo for having the most asymmetrical technicolour mind known to man and for making this book a billion times better than anything we could have done without him.

Rick for showing Chris how to use a spreadsheet.

Everyone at Street Feast past and present for being great people to work with and changing the way people consume food in London.

Dong and Plamen for being total pros in the kitchen and bossing it week in, week out.

Number 3, Jim, Pat and Purple Haze for the early days.

Ian Warren, James George, Matt Chatfield and everyone at Cool Chile and all of our suppliers who make our produce that much better.

Disco Dan, The V Man, Raquel, Pablo and the rest of the breddos who showed up (and paid) weekly for tacos in the early days.

The regulars at Netil Market who sustained our business for so long (especially you, Hoops).

Sarah, Helen and especially Romilly at Quadrille for the incredible opportunity to publish this book and for putting up with our weirdness.